# Caroline Chisholm:
# The Emigrant's Friend

# Caroline Chisholm:
# The Emigrant's Friend

*Joanna Bogle*

First Published in 1993
Gracewing
Fowler Wright Books
Southern Avenue, Leominster
Herefordshire HR6 0QF

*Gracewing Books are distributed*

In New Zealand by:
Catholic Supplies Ltd
80 Adelaide Rd
Wellington
New Zealand

In Australia by:
Charles Paine Pty
8 Ferris Street
North Parramatta
NSW 2151 Australia

*In U.S.A. by*
Morehouse Publishing
P.O. Box 1321
Harrisburg
PA 17105
U.S.A.

*In Canada by*
Meakin & Associates
Unit 17, 81 Auriga Drive
Nepean, Ontario, KZE 7Y5
Canada

© Cover illustration: *Sydney in the Forties* by J Fowles
© Half-title illustration is taken from
*Advance Australia, Caroline Chisholm*, London 1852
by Thomas Fairfield after portrait by A C Hayter.
Both illustrations courtesy of The State Library of
New South Wales, Macquarrie St, Sydney, Australia.

ISBN 0 85244 205X

Typesetting by Action Typesetting Ltd, Gloucester
Printed by The Cromwell Press,
Broughton Gifford, Melksham, Wiltshire SN12 8PH

# Contents

To my dear parents in law,
Brigadier & Mrs B L Bogle,
with love & thanks for so many things

# Author's Introduction

Many years ago I read in a children's magazine a splendid story about a lady in a crinoline and bonnet who helped poor people and who had a dashing soldier husband. The images stayed in my mind: the lady dancing with some children on the deck of a ship, and offering shelter to a small ragged orphan in what looked like a converted barn.

Later, when I visited Australia, I was enchanted to find this lady on the back of the five-dollar note. She was Caroline Chisholm, heroine of Australia's pioneering days, and stalwart campaigner on behalf of emigrants to that country. I read about her, researched her life story, became more and more fascinated, and then determined to make her better known in England, the land of her birth.

Mrs Chisholm is commemorated by a plaque on the house where she lived in Islington, in North London. There she interviewed and helped many prospective emigrants and a number of distinguished people including the novelist Charles Dickens. In Australia, a school and a social welfare society bear her name. More recently she has become the object of some controversy, as her picture was removed from the new-style redesigned $5 banknote. In contrast the Queen was retained on the note, and campaigners who feel that Australia should no longer be ruled by a Monarchy have taken up Mrs Chisholm as a symbol. Caroline herself would probably have been some-what bemused by this as she was not only a modest person, but was also the staunchest of monarchists, and a firm believer in the strongest possible links between Australia and Great Britain — a subject which she very frequently brought into her public speeches and writings.

Yet whatever one may think of this recent controversy her

story does deserve to be better known, and her true role in history recognised. Her life has many useful messages for today, and I hope that this book will resonate with all those who are looking for answers to many of the same problems she faced some 250 years ago.

I must thank my husband, Jamie, for first encouraging me to write this book. I am also grateful to the staff at Australia House in London, the Public Records Office at Kew, the London Library, the Catholic Central Library, and the India Office Record Office.

# Prologue

In 1838 a young couple and their children were among the passengers disembarking from a ship, the *Emerald Isle*, in Sydney Harbour, in the colony of New South Wales. The ship had already docked at Adelaide and at Hobart, so the passengers had seen something of Australia. Now they were in the colony's busiest port, and looking eagerly around at the town which had grown up around it. Convicts had been shipped here in misery for decades, but now the system of transporting criminals had ended, and the population of Sydney included many free settlers, together with traders, soldiers, explorers and the government officials needed to administer this emerging colony.

Caroline Chisholm's arrival on Australian soil was in fact a decisive moment in the history of the colony − although neither she nor her Highland-born Army officer husband Archibald could possibly have imagined this.

She was a young woman of thirty years of age, the mother of two small boys, and with the experience of several years as an Army wife in India behind her. Quietly spoken and rather attractive with large eyes and light brown hair under her shady bonnet, she did not seem a remarkable person. Together with her husband, she spent the first hours on arrival in Sydney attending to domestic arrangements: a room for the night, a meal for the children, long-terms plans to discuss now that the journey was over. Army connections meant that it was not difficult to make contacts and fit into the modest social life of this growing colony. The future, however, was to bring much more.

Mrs Chisholm was the first person to recognise the specific human problems of emigrants to Australia, and to set about tackling them with common sense and determination. It was her waggon trains criss-crossing the bush country that settled young people on farms where jobs and friendship were to be found, it was her untiring efforts to lobby the colonial government in London that brought about changes in official attitudes towards the Australian colonies, and it was her sympathy and human warmth that enabled the poor and the hopeless of the old world to view emigration not as a miserable necessity but as something offering the hope of a better future.

Unlike her contemporary Florence Nightingale she lacked any useful political and social influence. She was working and campaigning in an obscure corner of the globe, in a territory regarded as a place of loneliness and exile. Her essentially practical outlook enabled her not only to overcome difficulties but to speak effectively in terms that people could readily understand, opening up the idea of a free and happy country teeming with opportunities and enterprise.

In an important sense, Caroline Chisholm was to give Australians the basis of a new and lasting national identity. The brutality, horror and loneliness of the early days gave way to the notion of a 'lucky country', a place where families could prosper, a nation founded on teamwork, co-operation, optimism, and family life.

She brought to her chosen task the quiet faith of one who disliked a parade of piety, but who was nevertheless profoundly motivated by a deep belief in God and in His Providence. In this, she was before her time, as she lived in an age when sectarian controversies were rife. She was similarly before her time in her assertive and confident uses of the public arena as her own territory: she saw nothing strange in a woman taking up a cause and tackling major projects with enthusiasm and satisfaction.

Yet if her finest achievements were to be in Australia her story did not begin there. Indeed, few things could have seemed less likely, at her birth, than that her face would one day appear on an Australian banknote, or that her name would appear in the standard history and reference books on that country.

Life for Caroline Chisholm began in a farming family in

Northamptonshire, in an England still not yet industrialised. At that time the stage coach was the only means of travel to another city, and longer journeys belonged strictly to the highly adventurous. Yet Australia was not the first far flung land Caroline was to visit, and if we are to understand her character it is with parochial Northamptonshire that we must start.

# Chapter One

# How it Began

Visitors to Northampton today find a busy town dominated by a modern shopping precinct and office blocks. The city exudes an air of prosperity and commerce. Traffic is excluded from the shopping precinct, but hurtles round its edges, whirling around Holy Sepulchre Church and out along the main road past the Catholic Cathedral.

It is a town of some 180,000 inhabitants. Wide roads curl around the town's outskirts, carrying the shop and office workers out into homes in the suburbs. Northampton was declared a New Town in 1968 and subjected to enormous rebuilding projects in the 1970s and '80s. You have to hunt to find the traces of history that still abound: the picturesque Market Square, some fine churches; and links that go back to the days when shoes for Cromwell's Army were manufactured here, or to when the first market charter was granted back in the 12th century.

However two hundred years ago things were very different. Northampton was then primarily a market town which acted as a focus for the neighbouring agricultural area. The streets would have been muddy and rutted, and along them would have trundled not cars and lorries, but carts and heavily-laden horses − and the busy feet of country folk used to hard work on the land.

In the 1800s the population of Northampton was a few thousand people; the railway had not arrived − or even been thought of! It was to make its appearance in 1845. The various industries which were to make the town's name as a manufacturing centre had not yet been created. Only the shoe and leather industries, which dated well back into history, were present. The great Industrial Revolution was yet to come.

1

Northampton was the same as it had been for 100s of years. It was in this country town that Caroline was born, the daughter of William and Sarah Jones.

In 1796 William Jones was a pig-dealer owning property at Mayorfold in the town centre. His name appears in the Poll Book for that year. Northampton returned two members of Parliament and in the election Mr Jones, 'hog dealer' was listed as having voted for the Hon Spencer Perceval and Mr William Walcot – no secret ballot in those days!

Later, presumably when his family increased, he moved out to Wootton, just on the town's outskirts. It lies across the River Nene from Northampton, beyond Cotton End and Hardingstone. Its name simply means 'a farm by the wood', from the Saxon 'wudu tun', and over the years it had been spelt Witone, Wutton, Whutton and Weton. It was here, in 1808, that Caroline Jones was born, a healthy and welcomed baby for William and his wife Sarah. The date was May 30th. Caroline was the youngest in a large family. The sister nearest to her in age, Harriet, was four years her senior. It was a happy home. Caroline's father was in his sixties when she was born, but his wife at 37 was much younger. The family was prosperous, playing an active part in the life of the local area.

On 26th June the baby was taken into Northampton to be baptised at Holy Sepulchre Church. It was an historic setting for this event in the life of a tiny baby who would herself contribute a special chapter to her country's history. The church – known locally as 'the Round Church' – is one of only five in England modelled directly on the Holy Sepulchre itself in Jerusalem, perhaps the most famous being the Temple Church in London. The entrance is through a 14th-century porch, and inside monuments and stained glass reflecting the passing centuries of Northampton life look down on the worshippers.

Northampton has a strong Protestant and Evangelical tradition – it had been a Puritan stronghold in the Civil War and had lost its castle because Charles II ordered it to be destroyed on his Restoration. The faith into which baby Caroline was baptised seemed simple and straightforward. There was not a great deal of religious controversy among yeoman farming families such as the Jones. They were devout members of the Church of England, worshipping regularly according to the set forms of the Book of Common Prayer. They were familiar with the Bible and held daily family prayers. Caroline was brought up to know the Lord's Prayer and some of the psalms by heart, and was expected to learn her catechism, and would be told Bible stories and encouraged to read the Bible herself. The Ten Commandments were regarded as the basic code of life, and children were taught them and expected to obey them.

Caroline grew up in a cheerful, united, hard-working family. There was enjoyment of good food, home-grown or home-raised, spread regularly on the family table. There were games and endless opportunities for good fun with her brothers and sisters. The Jones family were well liked locally, and popular — regarded as good employers and good neighbours.

William Jones was able to provide well for his family, and home life also included a good education for all the children. As Caroline grew older, there would be lessons that included French — in which she became fluent — and music, as well as a good grounding in literature. There was also a strong sense of history and tradition pervading her home — she grew up with a sense of pride in being British, and in her country's achievements and heritage.

At this time King George III was on the throne — a more popular monarch than his two predecessors George I and George II, because he appeared more English. The German Hanoverian kings had not been much loved by those they were sent to rule in Britain in order to preserve the Protestant ascendancy from the Catholic Stuart claims, however 'Farmer George' was generally accepted. The Stuart cause was seen as lost. George III was identified with the popular notion of 'John Bull', the sturdy, independentminded, family-based Englishman who enjoyed the outdoors and loved his country with a straightforward patriotism. He and his queen, Charlotte, had fifteen children, of whom the oldest acted as Regent during the king's bouts of porphyria and related insanity. The Prince Regent, the future George IV, was not popular, and tales of his wild spending, immoral lifestyle and dislike of his father were widespread.

At the time of Caroline's birth Britain had been engaged for many years in war with France — first following the French Revolution and then continuing with the advent of Napoleon. The news from the battlefields on the continent was followed by the people back at home via the newspapers — in Northampton, the *Northampton Mercury* and the *Northampton Herald* filled their front pages with the latest despatches as well as with the political news from London. Families also had their own contacts abroad — notably with the American colonies where so many Englishmen had settled and were sending back news of their exploits.

Caroline was to have a fairly typical Georgian childhood, typical for the product of a reasonably well-to-do farmer. Fun and companionship with a large number of brothers and sisters, a strong message of pride in country, a personal identification with the town of her birth and its surrounding countryside, and an organised routine of household duties, solid meals, Sunday worship, and seasonal festivities.

However into this routine existence came occasional surprises. One was to have a profound effect on Caroline, and to form one of her earliest and most vivid memories. It happened when she was still very tiny. The family heard a noise of shouting and loud laughter from the road that ran along by the farmhouse, and went out to investigate. Some local boys had come across a stranger in the street and were shouting, throwing sticks and insulting him. When Farmer Jones moved in to rescue him they warned him off, explaining that the man was a Frenchman, and a dangerous one at that — a Roman Catholic priest whom they were hounding out of Wootton as quickly as they could. The elderly foreigner was already splattered with mud and filth, his tired and lined face showing exhaustion and confusion. William Jones took him by the arm and led him back to the house, telling the rough local lads to leave him alone.

The Frenchman was indeed a priest, elderly and far from home. He was one of several who had been forced to flee from France at the Revolution, and had arrived in England only to find a less than hospitable greeting as he went from place to place visiting the various scattered Catholic families. He was on his way to a distant family when he was passing the Jones' house. As it was already late in the day they invited him to eat with them and stay the night. It must have been a joy to him to discover that the older daughters of the family were quite proficient in French — the tiny Caroline would herself learn it from the same governess one day — and that all were keen and interested to hear news from France and to get a glimpse of that wider world beyond the confines of Northamptonshire life.

Of course they already knew about the French Revolution, and the causes of the current war with France that had been raging for so long. William and other local farmers had often discussed these things, and as patriotic Englishmen saw France as a hotbed of danger and intrigue that threatened the security and peace of their own much-loved country. They were grateful for the stability of their own nation, and more than willing to ensure its defence against aggressors. It must therefore have been exciting to hear first-hand information about what life in France was actually like. Now they could hear about the Revolution which had caused such havoc and terror, and about the disruption to normal life and to hopes of prosperity and peace for ordinary French people. The Jones family saw in this elderly priest a victim of The Terror, and of Napoleon's militarism. The latter had come to be known as 'old Boney' and was a bogey-man in popular folklore in England ('Boney will get you!', parents used to say to naughty children).

The old priest was gentle and courteous, grateful for the hospitality offered and anxious not to outstay his welcome. The Jones', however, pressed him to remain with them until he was fully rested and able to continue on the next stage of his travels. In the end he made quite a prolonged stay with them, and became a loved member of the family circle. He became particularly fond of Caroline, the smallest member of the family, who when the others were busy at household tasks, school lessons or farm duties, was able to be a companion for him. She liked to hear him tell stories with his soft accent, and to chatter back to him about her own plans and activities. He had his own special seat near the fire in the evenings and she enjoyed the privilege of sitting down beside him to talk through the day's events before wishing him goodnight and being taken up to bed.

When eventually he moved on, he was warm in his thanks to Farmer Jones and all his family. Caroline never forgot the gentle touch of his hand on her head as he imparted a blessing on leaving, telling her parents that he had come to love all their children and would miss them very much 'especially this dear little child'. From now on, if ever anyone tried to convince her that Catholics were strange, sinister, wicked people she would know that it was nonsense. She felt that a Catholic priest was a man of God, and someone kind and good.

The old priest was not the only stranger to receive a welcome at the family farm. The next was also someone who was a victim of war, and who brought its reality into their domestic circle. This time it was a badly wounded soldier, home from the war, but unable to work because he had lost a leg and moved about awkwardly on a crutch. Like the old abbé, he had been found on the road, and brought in for a meal and a rest. His wound troubled him a good deal, and for a long time he had to be nursed carefully. It was while he was sitting with a blanket over his lap, slowly regaining his strength, that he would talk about his experiences − not only of the present war, but of the wider world where he had travelled and seen service. Caroline had only the haziest ideas of geography. It was exciting to discover about places that were hot and exotic, full of promise and adventure. Perhaps it was this soldier who first gave her the notion that it was by travelling overseas that people could improve their lot, and leave behind the troubles and difficulties of a struggling life.

Later, and probably with hindsight, she was to recall a satisfying game in which she filled a basin with water and set it in the middle of a bed to be an ocean. Then she made some of her collection of small wooden dolls wait at one end while others were sent over the water to them in a boat. Remembering the old French priest, she was determined to have religious tolerance, and decided that one of the small figures was a Wesleyan minister and another a Catholic priest. Once settled in their new land they prospered − she had them sending a little pile of wheat in a thimble back across the sea. But the game ended in a mess − the bed's soft base was not a secure place for a great bowl of water and it overturned. Disaster! Water splashed everywhere, soaking the quilt and mattress, and dripping on the floor. Grown-ups suddenly arrived in great profusion. Hands descended, whisking away quilts, administering punishment, and swiftly removing the dolls and bowl. Caroline wept as she was briskly punished, and after that the game was forbidden – she only managed to play it again by doing it in a dark cellar with a rushlight.[1]

Caroline was a sturdy, self-reliant child, intelligent, happy and suffering from no serious childhood illnesses. Her small world was secure. It was full of colour, richness and interesting things. The only upsets were mild domestic ones. When she began to take lessons, she enjoyed them and found studying stimulating. Although life was ordered and sometimes strict – this was not a home where rudeness, disobedience or childish tantrums would be tolerated – on the whole there was plenty of fun and laughter. Later, when she herself was running a school for little girls, she tried to put into practice the methods and systems she had known in her own childhood. She always felt that children should be taught by encouragement and example, and allowed to participate in practical things and not merely learn by rote. In her own childhood, punishments were rare and always fairly administered. The cane was there, but the emphasis was on showing children how to avoid it rather than on constantly threatening its use.

Above all, hers was a country childhood. Many times, in later years, she would return in her talks and campaigning work to the immense benefits of growing up amid fields and fresh air, with good food and wide open spaces. 'A rural childhood sanctifies childhood, gives an industrious stimulus to the young, and a certainty of home to the aged' was how she was later to express it. She qualified this by emphasising that she was not urging that everyone should be a farmer, but merely arguing that if a man could be allowed to own just a tiny plot of land on which to have a home for his family, he would thus be allowed the dignity of seeing them grow up in relative comfort and good health, away from the humiliation and dangers of life among the impoverished city poor.

Sunday church attendance was at the time a standard part of life, but perhaps the small Caroline found its formality, and the length of the sermons, rather a trial. God must have seemed rather remote and far-away as the congregation sat stiffly in the high-backed pews and listened to the clergyman preaching. Wriggling and fidgeting and signs of boredom were not allowed, and although it felt good to be sitting there in Sunday-best clothes there was not much to interest or stimulate a lively little girl. She knew about God, and recognised Him as the Creator of everything, and had no desire to rebel against Him – but in church He seemed to be a rather bleak figure. No wonder people were turning so enthusiastically to the new Methodism as a challenging alternative! The Church of England disapproved of Mr John Wesley's preachings, and frequently reminded its congregations that their duty was simply to attend the church of their baptism, and not to go astray. But at the same time, with rare exceptions, the Anglican Church gave them little spiritual food. These were the days of matins and very formalised preaching as standard fare. Holy Communion was rarely celebrated and not a regular part of church life for most people. Caroline's faith probably developed more at home, with bedtime prayers in an intimate environment.

The only sorrow that was to mark Caroline's childhood came when she was six. Her father died after a short illness. The *Northampton Mercury* for April 16th, 1814, recorded the event in its 'Deaths' column: 'On Tuesday last, aged 72, Mr Jones, pig-dealer, of this town. He has left a widow and twelve children to lament their irreparable loss.' He had been loved by all his children and Caroline was the baby with whom there was naturally a special bond. Holy Sepulchre Church was packed for his funeral and his body was laid in the churchyard in the heart of the town. He had had many friends, and his generosity and tolerance were known and respected. His widow was much pitied and friends and relations rallied round to help. The family business would carry on under the direction of Caroline's brothers. She knew that she must now try to be more of a companion and help to her mother, who would be lonely and sad. In fact they were to become very close and to remain good friends for the rest of their lives.

The same newspaper which had noted her father's death was also reporting great news in the development of the war and hailing – though a little prematurely as it turned out – the final victory over Napoleon. In fact that was not to come until Waterloo in 1816. The victory in 1814 was to prove illusory, but that did not stop the *Mercury* gloating about it: 'The Deliverance of Europe is accomplished – the Peace of the World is restored; and the dynasty of Napoleon has ceased to oppress mankind, and all this achieved without further bloodshed ...' There was even a poem about it, reflecting the widespread patriotism of the age:

'England, like the bird of Noah
Safely born the waves above
By heroic perseverance
Gains the branch of Peace and Love'.

These were not easy years in the English countryside. When the war did finally end, poverty and unemployment grew steadily. The harsh laws of the day put a high priority on preserving order, but there was rather less emphasis on any attempt to alleviate distress or to tackle its causes. Punishments for crime were savage. It was possible to be transported to Australia – a terrifying prospect as many people died during the harsh voyage – for quite minor crimes. The gallows remained the even grimmer prospect for crimes that were hardly more serious. The Church seemed remote from many people's lives in terms of actually contributing a note of tenderness or compassion. Individual Christians tried to show care and neighbourliness to those in need but organised benevolence was no part of standard parish life. Too often, the poor had simply nowhere to go if they lost their jobs and were turned out of their homes because they were unable to pay the rent. Those with large families to feed could easily be tempted to turn to crime. Richer people too often cocooned themselves from such harsh realities and preferred to ignore them.

Caroline was by now sharing regular lessons under a governess with her cousins. She was also beginning to enjoy music and dancing. However, the family tradition of help to those in need continued. Routine domestic duties with her mother included giving food and aid to anyone who came knocking at their door asking for it. The idea was to try to give such help with cheerful goodwill and a spirit of genuine friendship and service. She knew that this was a way not only of honouring her father's memory but of sharing something that should surely be the birthright of all — basic nourishment and shelter.

She had her share, too, of ordinary domestic tasks. The Jones' kept servants to help run the large household, but all the daughters helped with things: the bottling and preserving of fruit and the making of jams and jellies, making special dishes for particular occasions, the supervising of the domestic accounts and the ordering of provisions. All her life, Caroline was to see the smooth running of a large household as a task worthy of an intelligent woman's interest and enthusiasm, and to recognise the pleasure and quiet authority that went with it.

Idleness was not encouraged in a household that recognised the need to keep abreast of tasks that needed to be done — fruit picked and food preserved in the right seasons, and nothing wasted that could be put to good use. Caroline was kept busy and she enjoyed it. When she thought about her own future she had no fantasies about wanting to live in a palace and have a life of luxury. However, the world beyond Northampton held a fascination for her. The old French priest and the disabled soldier had opened her mind to this wider world at a very impressionable age, and she was very keen to travel. She had also taken to heart all the lessons that her parents had taught her about the importance of helping others. As she grew into her late teens she became more curious about what she could contribute to the world beyond her comfortable home.

**Notes**

1. Eneas Mackenzie *Memoirs of Mrs Caroline Chisholm*, London 1852.

# Chapter Two

# Archibald

In 1828 Caroline was twenty. She had grown into a good-looking girl, with glossy brown hair, a good complexion, and unusually beautiful large serious eyes. These gazed out on a world that she was eager to encounter. As the youngest of a large and boisterous family, she was not short of friends, and was popular in her social circle. In the normal course of events, it was this circle that would dictate her future. Her older sisters were already married and had children of their own. Her own life would surely follow the same pattern. She had been well trained and educated and was now ready to run her own home and to take on the responsibilities of a husband, family, and property.

The sons of the local farmers, however, busy with their talk of stock prices and crops, failed to attract her interest and attention. She would never admit that she was bored with them − and yet the idea of settling down and marrying one of them was not what she wanted there and then.

She had a longing − rarely expressed because there was no realistic chance of it being fulfilled − to travel and see strange and exciting places. She was also very anxious to help the suffering people that she knew existed outside her own circle. Already, she and her mother were known for their practical and neighbourly help for the poor. She felt that she would like to do more. When she thought about marriage, she felt trapped by the thought of a smug domesticity that excluded wider concerns. She did not particularly care for a smart house, a reputation for a good table, or days of gossip and shopping. If she married, she wanted to be able to run a home that would be open to those in need, full of life and activity and not merely a shrine to personal contentment.

Officers from the Army barracks at Weeden were a most welcome addition to the social scene of Northampton, and the young ladies of the town were always interested to see a new face at a social event. It was at a ball attended by a group of officers that Caroline Jones was first introduced to Lieutenant Archibald Chisholm.

A softly-spoken Scot with a pleasant Highland lilt to his voice, he brought with him all the romance of the Indian Army. He was tanned from his years of service abroad, but beneath this there was a pallor to his skin – like so many others who had served in India he had been unwell several times during his course of duty and was now at home enjoying a long period of leave in order to recover his strength.

His talk was not of local news but of that exciting, wider world with which Caroline had always longed to have some link. In answer to her questions he told her about India – land of spices, wars, exotic lifestyles and languages.

As she got to know him better, she discovered much more about him that made him stand out from all the other young men she had ever met. For one thing, he was something of a scholar. He enjoyed reading Greek and Latin – and was also fluent in Gaelic. His religion also set him apart – he was a Roman Catholic, and although to some people in Northampton that might make him an object of some suspicion and even derision, to Caroline it evoked memories of the old French priest of her childhood.

It was an adventure for her to take up the suggestion that he might teach her Greek. It gave him, at all events, a good reason for asking her mother if he might call. Mrs Jones, perhaps already a trifle worried about Caroline's lack of interest in the local eligible young men, was not at all displeased.

She was happy to see the amiable Lieutenant Chisholm – a man of poise and charm, of a good family and with a sound Army background – taking an interest in her daughter.

Archibald Chisholm was born on 15th February 1798, making him ten years older than Caroline. He came from a family that had proud traditions. Central to this family heritage was an attachment to the old Roman Catholic faith. Records show that as far back as 1579, at the height of the penal times when to practise this faith brought severe punishment, 'Thomas Chisholm Laird of Strathglass, was summoned before the Court for his adhesion to the ancient creed.'[1] When Archibald was born in the family home at Knockfin, Strathglass, family tradition and folklore had passed on much about the Chisholm links with the old church. Archibald was baptised the day after his birth, in the family chapel at Fanaskyle. His parents were John and Jean Chisholm (formerly Fraser). The chapel had been built in a secluded place so that its users could feel safe from any official interference, and around it had grown a substantial Catholic community. A book on *'The Catholic Highlands of Scotland'* published in the mid-19th century notes with perhaps a hint of smugness that 'the chapel was situated where it could only be approached by the road leading from the lower end of Strathglass, eighteen miles distant. This will, no doubt, account for the fact that while the entire territory northwards, and other adjacent districts, with a few exceptions of modern date, embraced and still cling to the innovations of the so-called Reformation, the inhabitants of Strathglass should from a comparatively remote period form so singular a contrast by their uniform adherence to the Catholic faith. It is amongst the earliest recollections of the oldest people yet living (1846) that a native Protestant could hardly be met with in this district.'[2]

Officiating at Archibald's baptism was the priest of the Strathglass mission in what was officially the parish of Kilmorack, the Revd Austin McDonald of Aigus. The witness was Archibald's uncle, William Fraser. This uncle was to play an important part in Archibald's life, as his father died while Archibald was still a small child, and William Fraser became his guardian.

The Chisholm clan was originally of Lowland origin, but had become virtually Gaelic by descent. Their badge was a fern and their ancient family fortress was Erchless Castle in Strathglass.

Archibald grew up speaking Gaelic as well as English. He had two older brothers, Aeneas and Colin, and a younger half-brother, Thomas. They were proud of belonging to the Chisholm family and clan. The head of the family was known as 'An Siosalach', 'The Chisholm', by ancient right. Being Catholic also gave them a special identity. Within living memory, as they were growing up, there had been active persecution of Catholics and they knew they were viewed with official disapproval. There were tensions too with the local Calvinist denominations: these were not ecumenical times. The records of the local Presbytery, or committee of the Presbyterian Church, show that in 1743, some 50 years before Archibald's birth, it was reported: 'The Presbytery do appoint their Commissioners to the ensuing General Assembly, to lay before the said Assembly the following brief representation respecting the state and growth of Popery in their bounds, particularly that the Presbytery do find ... Mr John Farquharson a Jesuit Priest, who, for several years, resided and traffick'd in the Chisholm's country as a Poppish Missionary ...' The report urged that the full force of the law be brought against John Farquharson and other Catholic missionaries and that the General Assembly 'protect the Protestant religion in their bounds, and discourage, by all reasonable and likely means, the Roman Catholic religion.'

The Chisholm family boasted two priests who were to become famous in the Catholic history of the Highlands, the 'fair bishops', John and Aeneas Chisholm. Archibald's brother was named after the latter. The Bishops were Vicars Apostolic of the Highland District – this was in the days before the Catholic church was able to establish a proper hierarchy and had to run the area as mission territory. Father John Chisholm had worked as a priest in Strathglass for several years when he was consecrated bishop in 1792. He handed over his Strathglass work to his brother Aeneas who in 1793 arranged for Father Austin McDonald to be appointed to help him. It was this Father McDonald who baptised Archibald Chisholm, in the chapel at Fasankyle which had been rebuilt and extended by Father Aeneas.

The family also had a strong military tradition. Even though they were sometimes persecuted for their religious faith at home, they were prepared to defend their country's interests abroad. It was entirely in keeping with his family tradition that the young Archibald should plan to take up a career in the Army by applying for a cadetship in the rapidly expanding colonial territories acquired by Britain in India. His brother Aeneas was to follow another family tradition by becoming a priest, while Colin would in due course go into the law, and practise in Aberdeen.

Archibald was educated at Fortrose Academy. When completing his application form for the East India Company's army, he answered the question 'Of what nature has your education been' with 'Classical', and in fact he was to retain a lifelong interest in Latin and Greek literature. When this application was made in 1818 he had to provide evidence of his baptism – in those days, the nearest thing to a birth certificate (compulsory and organised registration of births in Britain did not start until the 1830s). It is noteworthy that in obtaining a certified copy of his baptismal certificate, he had it attested by a Minister, Simon Fraser, and two Elders, John Forbes and Donald McDonald, who were evidently unable to write, as they each made a cross instead. These crosses were in turn attested as genuine by Hugh Fraser, a Justice of the Peace.

By the time of this application, Archibald's parents were both dead, and where he was asked to state the 'profession, situation and residence' of his next-of-kin he described himself as being 'under the protection of my uncle William Fraser Esq of Culbokie.' It was this uncle who had formally nominated him to Charles Grant, one of the Directors of the East India Company, as a cadet in the Madras Infantry. Archibald was duly accepted into the company after the relevant enquiries had been made. To the question on the application form 'Do you believe that any person has received, or is to receive, any pecuniary consideration, or any thing convertible, in any mode, into a pecuniary benefit, for your nomination?' he answered emphatically 'Certainly not.' All was evidently in order, and the form was dated 12th May 1818. He was appointed an Ensign on 3rd June and arrived in Madras on 29th September of that year.

The British were by then well established in India, although the country was not yet deemed to be part of the British Empire in a formal sense – indeed the expression 'British Empire' was not yet in common use. The country was instead run under the control of the East India Company, and the Madras Infantry was part of its Army. It was a forerunner of the great Indian Army which was to play such a major part in the country's history.

This was a savagely different world from the Scottish Highlands. It was a place of tremendous heat and uncertain native loyalties, of exotic sounds and smells and lifestyles, of terrible diseases and fascinating but difficult languages, of aching homesickness where colonists longed for news and letters from Britain. Archibald became a Lieutenant on October 30th, and was soon learning the skills necessary for this demanding and challenging life. One such was a reasonable proficiency in the Hindustani languages. Without this he would not be able to command effectively the men who would be placed under him.

After his initial training he was appointed to the 15th – it later became the 30th – Native Infantry. He was to see action with this unit in the First Burma War of 1824–26. He was also for a time Quartermaster and Paymaster to the Regiment.

Home leave was granted only every few years, and could be cancelled in time of war. Even leave back to the Madras Presidency from the front-line areas could be cancelled if native unrest threatened. Archibald experienced having half his leave cancelled in 1824 when he was suddenly summoned for duty in the Burma War. When he was finally granted a furlough back home to Britain in 1828 it was nearly ten years since he had seen his home. He had seen action and earned a medal. He had matured from a boy into a man, acquired a taste for travel and learned about coping with hardship and disease. He would bring home with him a new and wider perspective on life than he had gained from his boyhood in the Highlands. He also brought an understanding of the rapid changes that were coming with regard to Britain's role in the world. The large overseas territories that she had acquired through trade were opening up new possibilities for all her people. With the Napoleonic Wars behind her, she would now increasingly look beyond Europe for her spheres of influence. Already, her position in India was changing and consolidating itself. He would have a lot to talk about when he got back on home soil again.

His leave was granted on 22nd January 1828 and he sailed on 24th February. The journey home took several weeks and the period of furlough was of reasonable length to accommodate this. People serving in India also needed a lengthy period at home in order to recover their health and strength after the years of service in the tropics. After the reunion with the family at home there would be opportunities to travel about and meet old friends, enjoy some social life and bask in the satisfaction of being a link with the exotic world of the overseas colonies.

After his first meeting with Caroline, Archibald spent as much time as he could with her during his stay at Weedon. The Jones family circle was hospitable and he was made welcome not only by Mrs Jones but by Caroline's married brothers and sisters. As the weeks went by with a round of pleasant social gatherings, there was a general sense of approval from the whole family. Caroline's brothers and sisters were happy at the prospect of seeing their youngest sibling happily settled.

But Caroline herself hesitated. When Archibald Chisholm asked her to marry him, she did not say 'yes' immediately. She had been thinking long and hard about the implications of being an Army officer's wife. Was it not very much a life of petty gossip and social niceties, of leisure and triviality with great stress on precedence and formality? Above all, was it not a life where her conscious sense of wanting to do something useful and to serve God and neighbour would be regarded as somehow rather eccentric? She wanted very much to marry and have a large family of her own – but not at the expense of her integrity. Her husband must understand that she wanted to form a partnership that would achieve something valuable. Would he let her have the freedom to do the sort of things she wanted to do? When he pressed her to give him a reply to his offer of marriage she told him to wait for a month, and to think it over. If he wanted a wife on the terms she had set out, then he could come back, and he would find her waiting.

Perhaps after she had sent him away she had doubts, and wanted to call him back, but this she could not do. She settled back at the old farmhouse to wait. There were questions and giggles and arch glances from cousins and girlfriends. There was sympathetic understanding from her mother with whom she always had an affectionate and humourous bond. There was perhaps just a hint of exasperation from siblings who wanted to see this rather determined young sister organised into a sensible new life. But for herself there was only waiting, and thinking, and some heartfelt little prayers that the right decision be made on both sides.

At the end of the month Lieutenant Chisholm came riding down the London Road to the Jones family home at Wootton, and Caroline was waiting. The smiles with which they greeted one another were the prelude to what was to be a long and happy marriage. They would always have a good understanding about the things that really mattered. This was to be a marriage that was based on genuine friendship and trust and enabled them both to keep their dignity and individual personality.

The wedding was fixed for Christmas. The year was 1830. It would be sensible to have the ceremony at a time when all the family would be gathered together. Archibald formally requested an extension of his leave, and it was granted until February with the possibility of further extension until June. Caroline began to work and plan for her future life in India. Part of this was fun – there was the wedding dress to make, the trousseau to arrange and organise. Other things were sadder to contemplate – leaving the only home she had ever known, saying goodbyes to family and friends in the knowledge that even letters would take months to reach them and that precious links would become stretched by distance.

In later years, when the Catholic Church in Britain was more structured and organised, Catholics refused to marry in Anglican churches and insisted on their own ceremonies. However, in 1830 the situation was such that Catholics allowed themselves Anglican weddings as the only practical way of ensuring that they could be married in the eyes of the law. Archibald and Caroline doubtless discussed the situation, and with it the question of her own long-term religious allegiance. But in the meantime there was the fun and excitement of a merry family occasion.

Holy Sepulchre Church was full of smiles and affection as Caroline was brought to the door as a bride on December 27th, 1830. This was a church which frequently saw military weddings. The Jones family were glad to have their youngest member married in style. Perhaps Mrs Jones shed a tear or two about losing her close companion — but she was pleased that Caroline was finding happiness with someone who so evidently suited her. For Caroline, there was the heart-wrenching feeling of leaving behind so much that had always surrounded her — but also the deep joy of being united with a partner who would not only be loving and protective but also full of understanding and common sense.

The *Northampton Mercury* for January 1st, 1831, duly reported the event in its 'Marriages' column: 'On Monday last, at St Sepulchre's Church, by the Rev Spencer Gunning (by permission of the Rev B. Winthrop), Captain Archibald Chisholm, of the Honourable East India Company's service, to Caroline, youngest daughter of the late Mr Wm. Jones, of this place.'

The front page of the newspaper was filled with reports of the Luddite rioting sweeping the countryside, as unemployed farm labourers smashed up the new threshing machines which they felt were making them redundant. It was reported that the Archbishop of Canterbury had been authorised to prepare special prayers 'on the subject of the troubled state of certain parts of the United Kingdom', and meanwhile a local farmer printed an anonymous appeal to the men to cease from their destruction and listen to reason. There was also news of another very topical subject — the plans to build a railway from London to Birmingham, which would mean crossing over land belonging to farmers around Northampton. The local landowners were infuriated, and holding protest meetings and rallies to argue that the railway would bring disaster to the farming community, splitting up fields and permanently separating whole tracts of countryside.

Yet for the Jones family and their friends, this Christmas wedding was a happy occasion. Captain Chisholm made a dashing figure in his bright uniform as he walked his bride down the aisle. Then there was the big wedding breakfast where everyone toasted the bridal pair, and the fun of all the trimmings — cake and laughter and speeches.

Much later, when all the celebrations were over, and the great job of packing and organising everything had been completed, it was time to say goodbye. The journey would be made in easy stages. For the first few months of their marriage, Caroline and Archibald would live at Brighton, while they waited for the ship that would take them to India.


**Notes**

1. *The Catholic Highlands of Scotland.* by Dom Odo Blundell OSB, Sands and Co, Edinburgh and London 1909.
2. Ibid.
3. Until 1837, the only legally valid marriage ceremony was one in an Anglican church, except for Jews and Quakers, who were permitted their own ceremonies. The new registration system introduced in that year allowed for a civil registrar to attend a Catholic ceremony and thus legalise it. Until then, Catholics generally went through two ceremonies, the Anglican one and then a Catholic one. It seems likely therefore that the Chisholms did this. I have not been able, however, to trace a note of their Catholic wedding. There was a Catholic mission in Northampton (it was started in 1825) with a Father W. Foley in charge — probably this was where Archibald Chisholm worshipped. It may be that the Rev B. Winthrop, mentioned in the local newspaper as giving special permission for the wedding, was a local Catholic priest.

# Chapter Three

# A Brighton Catholic

For Caroline, not only did marriage alter her status and give her a whole new role and way of life, it also whisked her miles from home on the start of a long journey that was eventually to take her to the other side of the globe.

As a first step, they travelled south – to Brighton on England's south coast. Everything was exciting to Caroline – leaving Northampton, travelling by slow stages along the roads through strange villages and towns; discovering new places; being introduced as 'Mrs Chisholm'.

Brighton was to be only a temporary home for them. As a coastal town, it was a good spot for an Indian Army officer to recover his full health after the rigours of tropical diseases, and to build up a strong constitution for the future. It was also close to London, from where they would start the long trip to India.

Perhaps they also chose it because it had become, through a curious chain of events, a centre for Catholics. The Catholic community in England was so small that all links between its members were valued, and the town may well have been recommended to Archibald by Catholic friends.

Brighton had been a tiny fishing village only a few decades earlier, a virtually unnoticed spot on the Sussex coast. It had a broad, pebbly beach, and no particular coves or natural harbours. Further along the coast, the land swept up to produce the spectacular Seven Sisters cliffs where the South Downs met the sea.

What had changed things was the discovery by the Prince Regent of its proximity to London. How convenient – to have an attractive seaside hideaway only a few hours gallop in a coach down the broad straight route from the capital!

21

Here he gradually installed his informal court. In due course his splendid folly of a Pavilion, built in a quasi-Chinese style, was to appear in the centre of the town, and a whole way of life based on parties and merrymaking was to develop there. The little fishing village virtually disappeared under the massive building of roads and squares of elegant houses, as fashionable people flocked to be part of the scene. Sea-bathing become popular – it was said to be good for one's health. Brighton began to have the reputation of being a racy, rather irregular sort of place, where respectable people could raise their eyebrows at the latest goings-on, and rumours could be spread about liaisons and affairs among the fashionable.

Then came its Catholic links. The Prince of Wales, before he became Prince Regent, had fallen in love with the twice-widowed Mrs Maria Fitzherbert, who unlike other ladies who had crossed his path and caught his eye, was a devout woman who had no intention of becoming his mistress. Sweet-natured and gentle, she had a dignity that rested on a sincere religious faith. She was a practising Catholic and refused to betray the principles of her Church in order to have a dalliance with a prince, even if her heart did make her want to surround him with love and affection. She offered him friendship and companionship, and was markedly different in all her personal lifestyle and manners from the sort of people with whom he habitually kept company. When finally he insisted that she offered him something more than mere friendship, she made it clear to him that this could never be possible outside the bounds of matrimony. She lived, with her adopted step-daughter, in a modest house not far from the Royal Pavilion in the centre of Brighton. She married the Prince there in 1772 in a short private ceremony before two witnesses. The Prince kept a lock of her hair in a locket around his neck until he died and always thought of her as his true and only wife, notwithstanding the ceremony he later went through with Princess Caroline of Brunswick.

It was Maria Fitzherbert who provided Brighton with its Catholic links. She attended Mass regularly, and together with other Catholics around the Royal circle, formed a small community that was able to sustain a chapel which became an established Mass-centre, unusual in Sussex at that time.

By the time that Archibald and Caroline Chisholm arrived in early 1831, Catholic life in the town was quite well established. It was a place where regular Mass attendance, together with Confession and all the services appropriate to the various festivals of the year, could be a normal part of life.

Things had changed for Catholics in the first decades of the nineteenth century. Following the various social changes that had begun as the Napoleonic War receded into the past, Catholic emancipation had finally been brought about, and the old days of active persecution had ceased. It was part of a new mood that was felt across the country in many different ways. 1830 had seen the death of George IV, who had finally succeeded his father after some years as Prince Regent. He had now in turn been succeeded by his brother as William IV. But William had no heirs. As Duke of Clarence, he had enjoyed a long liason with the actress Mrs Jordan, and had a large family of ten children, the Fitzclarences. But none of them could inherit the throne. George IV's only child, a daughter, by Caroline of Brunswick, had died as a young bride in childbirth. Thus the only heir was the daughter of another brother, the Duke of Kent. This was the young Princess Victoria, in whom the whole nation was now taking a close interest. If and when she succeeded to the throne, surely a whole new chapter in English history would begin. The Northampton newspaper which had reported the Chisholm wedding had contained, as it often did, pieces of news about her, describing her education, and noting that she was now being taught by English tutors rather than exclusively by German ones but that she still spoke English with a marked German accent.

The British people were investing many hopes in this young woman — those in Northampton were not unique in their wish that her accession, which could not be long delayed as her uncle William was neither young nor in particularly good health, would be the beginning of something wholly new. It was all a part of the sense of many fresh things happening: war with the French now safely in the past; new techniques in farming; the first appearance of mechanisation and industrialisation.

It was an exciting time to be a young married couple contemplating a whole new life together. Caroline had never travelled so far from home before – had never even seen the sea. Now she was contemplating the much longer journey all the way to India. Archibald told her as much as he could about the sort of life she could expect to lead there. He did his best to answer all her questions and to give helpful advice about the long journey ahead of them and the things she would need for a life in the heat and inconvenience of a distant continent. For Caroline, it seemed exotic and exciting. All her life she had been aware of this thrilling world that lay beyond the farm and local life – now she would be part of it. The very name 'India' conjured up adventure and glamour. Back in Northampton, the little luxuries that found their way into local shops and thence to the dining-room tables of the well-to-do had often come from India – tea, for instance, and spices. People who had a son who had gone out to make his fortune there or who was serving in the Army showed letters that spoke of Britain's growing prestige and importance in these distant territories. Here was a matter for pride, and for very great excitement.

The most important thing that happened, however, in this period of their lives, was the decision taken by Caroline to join the Catholic Church. It cannot have been an easy decision. Catholics were still regarded as a distinctly odd group of people. Their prayers were in Latin and not in English, and the Mass appeared to be a curious ceremony involving much muttering by a priest and much kneeling and fluttering through prayer-books on the part of the congregation. There were still prejudices about alleged Catholic involvement with various anti-government plots, and a fixed conviction that to be a Catholic was to be in league with foreigners and to have a strange allegiance to a foreign Pope who probably had designs on England's throne. English Catholics were, by and large, a small and tightly-knit group of people who intermarried and who kept their religious faith to themselves. Conversions were few. Catholic churches were now allowed to be built, and those that existed were discreet, small buildings in remote places. They were generally at the poor end of a town or on some land that had been acquired cheaply, perhaps because it had an unsavoury reputation. Priests were still trained abroad, and many of the old Catholic families who had kept the faith through a number of generations still sent their children abroad to be educated as a matter of course. Alternatively, they educated them at home with private tutors who were often priests and acted as chaplains to the scattered Catholics of the neighbourhood, offering Mass in a private chapel that served as a centre.

To become a Catholic required a certain amount of courage and a great deal of discussion. There must have been many questions to which Caroline sought an answer. The Catholic beliefs about the Eucharist − such an anathema to Protestants − would need careful explanation. So too, would the practice of confession, and the notion of devotions to saints.

Caroline's motives in becoming a Catholic may have been a little mixed. Perhaps the Chisholm family urged it on her − certainly it was unusual for one of their number to marry outside the old faith. Perhaps she was also influenced at a more profound level by Archibald's own personal faith and commitment to his beliefs. He was several years older than her and very well educated, presumably able to answer her enquiries and respond with information and knowledge that were beyond the scope of her own religious formation.

However, Caroline's reception into the Catholic Church was not a mere formality. She practised her faith with dedication for the rest of her life, even though it sometimes caused her difficulties when she was at the mercy of the prejudices of others. She seemed to find that her new-found Catholicism rested comfortably on the solid Evangelical background of her childhood, but doubtless adding to it the note of warmth and personal relationship with God that had been lacking in the stiff formality of the Anglican worship of the day.

Whenever Caroline was to speak about religion in later life, it was in language that would be easily understood by everyone. She was always to have a very strong conviction of God's Providence (a term she was fond of using) and was always to show immense tolerance − in an intolerant age − of other people's beliefs and ideas.

In her own private life, devotion to the Eucharist became central. She received Holy Communion regularly − and this was at a time when the Catholic Church's rules on the subject involved a profound spiritual preparation and fasting from midnight.

Catholics in Brighton had had a chapel of sorts since 1799, and now in the 1830s there was quite a thriving congregation. The Church of St John the Baptist would be formally consecrated in 1835 after Archibald and Caroline had left the town, but already a Catholic presence was very evident in the community. Maria Fitzherbert's quiet determination to practise her faith had had curiously long-lasting effects in this corner of Sussex.

There were no Catholic Bishops in England at this time, the country being run as a mission territory under Vicars Apostolic appointed by Rome. There was very little in the way of Catholic literature, and nothing that was aimed at achieving conversions. Instruction had to be by word of mouth, and the devotional life was assisted by old prayer-books that offered an old-fashioned approach based on a deep interior life and a sense of private reflection.

When Caroline became a Catholic she took the name Monica as her Confirmation name. Catholics had for a long time followed the practice of adopting a new name at confirmation, choosing a saint to whom they had a particular devotion. The idea would have been quite new to Caroline, and she would have been able to spend time and thought on it. In choosing Monica, she deliberately chose someone who would be a source of inspiration and encouragement to her in her job as wife and mother. Catholics regarded St Monica as the patron saint of mothers – she lived in the fourth century and was the mother of St Augustine, whose notorious lifestyle ended when he finally became a devout Christian and apologist for the faith. It was always said of Monica that it was her prayers and dedication that had finally saved Augustine, fulfilling the promise that had been made to her when she agonised about what was to become of him 'It is impossible that the child of so many tears should be lost.' That Caroline's devotion to St Monica was no superficial thing can be seen from the fact that in due course she was to name all her daughters after her – on each of their baptismal certificates Monica appears as the second Christian name.

The exact date of Caroline's reception into the Catholic church is not known, but it may have been on St Monica's day, August 27th, 1831. It may not have been at Brighton, for there is no record of it in the registers of St John the Baptist Church, which date back to 1797. It is possible that it had taken place previously in London, or some other place on the journey from Northampton after the wedding, for the journey would have been of several days' duration, with overnight stops in a number of places and possibly even a prolonged stay with friends or family. Indeed, there may even have been another post-wedding trip to Scotland, to meet all the Chisholm family as a new bride, where the ceremony of reception would have been particularly appropriate.

What is clear is that it occurred at some stage after her marriage and before the journey out to India. During the latter part of her time at Brighton she kept a diary, in which regular attendance at the Catholic church featured prominently.[1]

Archibald had succeeded in getting an extension of his furlough until June (1831) and then again until December of that year. When he finally returned to India Caroline went through a lonely period. She took drawing lessons, went to church, walked up and down the sea front, and wrote in her diary. Archibald sailed for India on the *Elphinstone*, which departed from London on 6th January 1832, under Captain J. Short. The *Madras Almanac* duly recorded the arrivals from Britain on May 14th including 'Lieutenant F. Chisholme (sic) Lieutenant F. Carter, Mr A. Macintire, cadet . . .'

Back in Brighton Caroline must have felt rather bleak. She had enjoyed one year of married life − just enough time to get used to its comforts and domesticity. Ahead of her lay the unknown adventure of the sea journey to India, and then the drama of life on that distant continent. Meanwhile there was this quiet little town by the sea, with not much to do except wait until her own travel arrangements were completed. Clothes had to be made and fitted, advice and information sought about what her future lifestyle might entail, and enquiries made to confirm shipping plans. However, she had plenty of time in which to think and speculate on what the future held, and perhaps to worry a bit about it. India was a place of colour, adventure and excitement − but also of disease and danger. Many of the young wives who went out to join their husbands there did not return. The hot climate with its dirt and disease exacted a terrible toll. Children born to such couples also faced a struggle to survive, and tales of sad deaths of small babies and of the loneliness and sorrow of their parents were beginning to be known in England. Families heading out to India were often admired rather than envied.

In the event Caroline had a year for such speculation. She was finally able to join Archibald in August 1833, having also made her passage on the *Elphinstone*. She arrived in Madras on August 4th of that year.

It was the start of a new chapter. And after a period of loneliness and perhaps boredom, she was at last to find a fitting challenge in life.

**Notes**

1. The diary is mentioned in *Caroline Chisholm*, by Margaret Kiddle (see bibliography). A later biography, *Fifty One Pieces of Wedding Cake*, by Mary Hoban, laments its disappearance.

# Chapter Four

# India

The meeting between Archibald and his bride at Madras must have been an emotional one. During the months of enforced separation each must have had many fears about the other's safety and well-being. He had left her as a young country girl, inexperienced and alone, to travel hundreds of miles to meet him. Meanwhile his own army duties involved him in the ever-present risk of danger.

Nothing in Northampton or Britain could possibly have prepared Caroline for the impact of India with its smells and its heat, its colour and contrasts of life and death on the streets of Madras. Beggars on the streets pleaded for alms as they exhibited all sorts of hideous diseases. Cows − deemed sacred by the Hindu religion − roamed at will. Exotic temples gleamed with treasures, and stalls sold sticky sweetmeats teeming with flies, or materials in richly glowing colours, or glittering ornaments and jewellery of design and style no European could have devised. The shouts and cries were in strange languages and intonations. The crowds teemed and jostled in the heat as British soldiers in red uniform, ladies with bonnets and parasols, and native Indians in every sort of traditional dress hurried about their business.

Caroline was joining the band of British people who had established a way of life for themselves in this ancient land while retaining a wholly British outlook and the closest possible links with home. It was a community which had a strong sense of mission − there was a growing awareness of the importance of India's position and of the role of the British in bringing Western influences in many fields of life. It was also a community that sensed its vulnerability. Although people were fascinated by the sights and sounds of India all

29

around them, they were also acutely aware of the constant clashes between the Indian and the European way of looking at things, and of the resentments and passions that lingered beneath the surface of an apparently reasonably smoothly-run territory.

European settlement in India had begun in the early part of the 16th century with the arrival of the Portugese. But although Portugal's influence was to be long-lasting in many respects, especially religious, it was really the coming of the British in the next century that had really shaped India's history in a concrete way.

It had happened almost by accident. The British set up trading posts and then created the British East India Company to protect and co-ordinate their efforts. It was this company, 'John Company', that was to set up a British administration which ruled India for many years.

Caroline would swifly learn of some of the tensions and anxieties that lay constantly beneath the surface of life in British India.

In 1756 the Nawab (local ruler) of the territory around Calcutta, Suraj ud Dalulah, had captured the British settlement there. His forces overran the settlement and packed all the captured British men − 146 in all − into a tiny prison cell just 18 feet by 14 feet one stifling summer night. In the morning only 23 staggered out alive. This was the notorious 'Black Hole of Calcutta'. The grim deaths were avenged by the arrival of a force from Madras led by the celebrated Robert Clive − 'Clive of India' and Admiral Charles Watson, who recaptured the settlement and forced Suraj ud Dalulah to sign a treaty giving back to the British all the privileges they had previously enjoyed. The Nawab had originally attacked Calcutta for fear of foreign aggression and because he claimed that the British had abused privileges and had fortified their local centres without permission. With his defeat at the hands of Clive, British authority was fully restored. Clive's subsequent victory at the Battle of Plassey consolidated this by squashing a further futile attempt by the Nawab to challenge British power in June 1757. But the 'Black Hole of Calcutta' would never be forgotten among the British in India. It had penetrated into the collective memory and remained as something that was passed on as a piece of history to each newcomer. It was spoken of with dread and used as a reminder of the sort of terror that lurked unless British rule was effectively and authoritatively affirmed and backed with military strength.

The East India Company's army was thus aware of its responsibilities. It trained its men and gave them a strong sense of duty and commitment. India was now governed under the provisions of William Pitt's India Act of 1784, and this would be the framework until things were changed by the events of the Mutiny in the 1850s.

There was a sense of missionary zeal among some of the British. In 1833 slavery was to be declared illegal throughout the British Empire – the result of the great crusade on the subject waged by William Wilberforce and his 'Clapham sect' of Evangelical campaigners in Parliament. But it was a long time before slavery died out in India. Much earlier, in 1795, there had been attempts by the British authorities in India to outlaw the practice of killing new-born baby girls, but it took a long time to eradicate, and infanticide continued to be practised for many decades. In 1829 the equally abhorrent practice of suttee – the burning of a young widow on her husband's funeral pyre – was declared illegal in Bengal. The British were appalled at the contempt for life that this abuse of young women showed. But stamping it out required firm measures and showed how deeply ran the different outlooks, how savage was the clash of cultures.

When Caroline Chisholm arrived in Madras she became part of an elite group – pioneers in a new way of life. They were the British wives of soldiers and officials who together with their husbands were forging a lifestyle and culture of their own in a strange and exotic land.

Madras was an ancient city, and full of the treasures of past centuries as well as the many trimmings of British rule. It was for many new young British wives an introduction to challenges and difficulties of a type unknown before. They had to tackle diseases and discomforts unknown to generations of their forebears. They had to wait for months for news of people they loved and had left behind in England – and also for new books, magazines, newspapers, and information on everything from fashion to events in the wider world. They had to contend with snakes and mosquitos, strange foods and blistering heat, and also with aching homesickness. They also discovered the thrill of magnificent landscapes, haunting strains of Indian music, and plants, flowers, and animals previously glimpsed only in encyclopedias or geography books.

It was for this that Caroline had accepted Archibald's offer of marriage and declined the attentions of Northamptonshire squires' and farmers' sons. Here at last was the wide and exciting world that she had pictured in her imagination as a child listening to an old soldier's tales or playing with dolls in toy boats in a basin full of water.

The Chisholms soon settled into the British community. Caroline took on the challenge of running a household of her own — and in such a completely alien environment. There were large numbers of native servants to carry out household tasks, all sorts of small social obligations to fulfil, and many things to arrange and organise so as to make life bearable and comfortable amid the heat and the great sense of isolation. Doubtless Caroline had much to tell her family in the letters that went back to Northampton — letters that took a very long while to arrive, but which would be passed around and read and re-read.

A newcomer was expected to find her rightful place in the British colony, and not to start making claims about the correct way to do things. She must learn through watching others, and sometimes also suffer from her own mistakes, as she sought to come to terms with established norms. Once a routine of life had been established, one major problem for the ladies was that of boredom. The oppressive heat prevented many activities. The officers' wives had their little social gatherings, the pleasure of exchanging news from home when it arrived, and of gossiping about the latest appointments or the trivia of local news. But unlike their husbands they had no specific duties, and with servants doing most of the actual housework, the days sometimes seemed long.

Things were very different for the wives and families of ordinary soldiers. Little if any provision was made for them in the scheme of things. The families seemed to have no official status at all — a soldier was somehow not expected to marry, and if he did his wife and offspring were expected to fend for themselves. Ignorant and unlettered, unable to enhance their lives by means of literature or training for a future trade or profession, the children ran wild. The boys were more fortunate than the girls, as they would probably follow their fathers into the Army. But the girls simply hung around the barracks, picking up swear-words and songs, playing in the dust and dirt, unwilling to return to drab stuffy homes where overburdened mothers struggled to cope with household tasks.

The British authorities, who saw the need to stamp out cruel practices among the native population, and to impose concepts of fairness and decency, seemed not to have noticed unfairness right on their own doorstep. There was no provision of any kind for the education of soldiers' daughters, even though their fathers were prepared to risk life and health in defence of British interests and showed pride and patriotism in their loyalty to their regiment and nation.

The future for such girls was a bleak one. Too often they ended up as 'barracks women', forming relationships with the soldiers while still in their teens, dying young of disease or perhaps bearing illegitimate offspring in shame and degradation.

A pamphlet published many years later honouring the work of Caroline Chisholm refers to ' ... temptations which assailed morality in the military stations at that time ... the almost entire absence of any adequate machinery for protecting the young'[2]. Soldiers were regarded as the raw material for keeping order among the native population, fighting border wars and upholding British interests. If they were themselves unruly or disobeyed orders, they were subject to the savage Army discipline of the day. But in the broader sense their homes and families were deemed to be of no concern to the military authorities.

Caroline recognised this unwholesome situation as soon as she became accustomed to army life in Madras. Brought up in her family tradition of practical help to those in need, she was keen to do something. Active philanthropy was not encouraged among the officers' wives, and she was probably regarded as more than a little eccentric when she raised the possibility of a small school for the soldiers' daughters. But it caught on, and within a few months was to become a reality, with the full backing of the authorities.

The aim of the school was to prepare girls realistically for their lives. Few had any idea of how to run a home or manage money. They lacked a sense of identity and purpose. The primary role of the proposed school was not to force them into classrooms and attempt to impose an academic curriculum, but to offer opportunities for them to learn skills and create a community together, so that they could cope effectively with whatever life brought.

Once use of a building had been obtained, a matron and teacher were appointed. The whole project was to be under Mrs Chisholm's explicit direction. The building was in the Black Town area of Madras, and it was announced that the children would be instructed in 'reading, writing, arithmetic, needlework and domestic management. Their religious instruction and moral conduct will be made an object of particular attention.' There was no compulsion of any sort to attend – the establishment was simply offered as an assistance to parents, who could make use of it if they wished. On the other hand, if a girl left once she had been enrolled, she would not be re-admitted. It was to be an establishment which had a certain status and was to be taken seriously.

Setting up and running the school gave Caroline her first opportunity to work independently and on her own initiative. Back at home in Northamptonshire, she had been hemmed in by the demands, and the protection, of a loving but old-fashioned family. Now at last she had the freedom, as a married woman with a home of her own, to use the talents for organisation and communication that she had always possessed.

The girls – and their families – needed a clear framework of rules in which to operate. A system of 'tickets' was devised, with girls forfeiting these for misbehaviour. A timetable was organised, designed specifically to fit in with the needs of Indian life, where the coolest part of the day was the early morning. Thus the regulations specified that the girls were to 'get up at an hour so as to be able to take some recreation in the cool of the morning, either on the Beach or Esplanade, they are first however (after having washed themselves) to say a short prayer, and after they have come in to say their regular morning prayers and then to have their breakfast.'

Each child had to arrive at the school bringing her own mug, plate, knife, fork, and spoon, plus a box for her clothes. There was a uniform, although this was not provided until they had worn out such of their own clothes as they had brought with them.

Caroline was nothing if not realistic. None of these children had ever experienced formal schooling, or been offered much in the way of moral formation. It would be necessary to ensure that everyone recognised that the school was a community which had its own authority and sense of purpose. She appealed to the children as soldiers' daughters to be proud of themselves and their families. Their mothers were to find the school a boon — if there was any trouble or illness at home, the younger children could be brought into the school while things were sorted out. The babies were used for child-care lessons, as were infants from the Regimental Hospital!

In a message to the girls, later quoted in her own memoirs, Caroline announced that once a month the school's list of punishments for various offences was to be read out. These make rather severe reading, but emphasise the strong moral message that was being inculcated. The aim was to get entirely away from the Army approach, in which rigid obedience to parade-ground orders too often masked a grim underworld of brutality, bullying and viciousness. Instead, the aim was to foster a deeper sense of morality, in which lying, fighting, and stealing were viewed with horror, while honesty and integrity were given a high priority.

Thus 'for telling an untruth' the punishment was 'to forfeit five tickets, and to be kept for that day separate from the other children in the schoolroom, that visitors may at once know the offender', with stealing to be punished in the same way. A second offence meant having to wear, in addition, some black bracelets that were evidently a special badge of dishonour. A child was to receive no punishment for breaking crockery if she owned up at once, but failure to do so meant forfeiting three tickets. Other girls who were 'parties to the concealment' were to receive the same punishment 'for conniving at trifles may in time lead to great crimes'. The school's food was evidently very good, because being made to skip a meal was the standard punishment for sulking, quarreling, or fighting, while a girl who refused to help make a pudding was 'not to partake of the same'!

Caroline's message to her pupils addressed them affectionately as 'my dear little girls' and urged them to good conduct so that their parents would be proud of them: 'I fancy I already hear your father say, in honest pride, that my girl can keep accounts, cook a dinner, and she is only fourteen years of age; and your mother says, yes, and make a shirt and cut it out as well if not better than I can'. In addition to the punishments listed, the school also kept a cane, and she referred to it briskly saying 'The Rod in appearance is quite frightful, and I think you will have the same opinion of it, and I trust you will look upon the bracelets with a determination never to wear them'. But she also had a much better way of helping them avoid punishment than mere exhortation. She promised that 'if at the end of one year the Rod has never been used, you shall have a day's holiday to bury or burn it, and that you shall invite your parents to be present on the occasion, giving them cake, etc, made by your own hands. When the Rod is fairly out of the house, the Rewards shall be distributed, and the ladies and gentlemen who have so kindly supported this institution shall be invited to attend at the distribution of the prizes . . .'[3]

There is, alas, no account of this festival day which it is to be hoped eventually took place!

The girls formed committees to work together for cooking and other subjects, and must have had fun carrying out their little tasks. One account reports making barley water and later a cup of tea for 'Mary McMillin, who is not very well'. She was later reported to be much better. Cold meat left over from a meal was made into a pasty for 'the poor blind woman' and tea was similarly distributed to the local poor. Breakfast was ready on time, and the dinner of mutton curry sounds as if it must have been tasty although there was a comment that the rice was over-boiled. There was a butcher's bill of four rupees, one anna and six pennies. The small team making these entries into the housekeeping book in June 1836 were aged 13, 12 and 8!

All of this required organisation, enthusiasm and dedication. Caroline herself read the girls' reports and made
comments ('What have you done with the butcher's receipt?
What use did you make of the boiled barley after pouring
off the water?'), but she now had family responsibilities of
her own as well. The *India Register* for 1837 listed under
its 'births' for May 1836 'at Madras, the lady of Captain
Chisholm, 30th regt, of a son'. This was young Archibald,
born on May 4th, a healthy baby who gave great joy to his
parents. The young father was now a Captain, having achieved
this rank on 8th April 1833. Serving with him in the same rank
were Charles Snell, John Wilson, Charles Daviniere, and John
Deane.[3]

By the next year the Chisholms were based at Bowenpilly,
where a further son was born to them on 5th September
(1837). This new baby was named William after Caroline's
father. But although their lives were happy and fulfilled, India
was taking its toll. Captain Chisholm's health was, in common
with that of so many others, beginning to fail. He was due
for some more leave. After an Inspection at Secunderabad
in December 1837 (during which it was noted on his Army
record, with approval, that he spoke 'Hindoostannee' a little)
he reported back to Madras and on 5th January 1838 was
given two years secondment leave.

They had been discussing this prospect for some time.
Caroline had loved her work for the school, which had
taught her a great deal and encouraged her in the idea that
there was a good future to be had in the Colonies. Why go
back immediately to England? While they were still young and
the world was opening up for them, why not explore further?
The new colonies of Australasia beckoned those who had a
taste for adventure. After much debate, they decided that the
period of leave should be spent in Van Dieman's Land or
New South Wales, on the coast of the great island continent
of Australia.

India had been a formative experience for Caroline. It had
developed her character, taught her that she was a person who
could easily adapt to change and make the best of things,
and above all encouraged her qualities of organisation and

leadership. She left behind a lasting achievement in her school. It had made a dramatic impact on the lives of many individual children, and had also changed attitudes and challenged preconceptions among many at a high administrative level. It was, in its own way, an example of the changes that were coming in British India.

The school was to flourish for some while after Caroline's departure, and to become a standard part of Madras life as 'The Female School of Industry for the Daughters of European Soldiers'.

Change was in the air in all of Britain's territories. Back at home a new age was dawning, with the accession to the throne of a young Queen. There was a sense of optimism and idealism. Social reform was under way in many areas of life. There was a longing to be distanced from older and less humane ways of doing things. Letters from home spoke of rapid developments. The railways were coming — protest meetings notwithstanding! The Evangelical revival had brought with it a concern for the poor, for improved education and a greater sense of Christian nationhood with a sense of purpose and duty. Aware of it or not, the British were embarking on a new era, one that was for ever to bear the name 'Victorian'.

Caroline's school had given her a taste for tackling social problems, and showed her that where a strong initiative was offered, people were prepared to follow. She had proved to herself that people responded well to appeals to their sense of responsibility. They enjoyed being asked to help with a worthwhile project, and the feeling of being part of something successful. She herself was not, she discovered, easily tired or defeated and had the ability to bring people together and ensure that difficulties could be overcome and proper attention given to forward planning.

It was, she felt, a good time to be a young married woman. The world seemed to be opening up all sorts of ways, and life was offering her adventures and possibilities that her mother had never known. Perhaps the advent of Queen Victoria's reign had helped to bring about certain changes of attitude. It had certainly provided a sense of swiftly-changing priorities, of new adventures and exciting times ahead.

It was as the young Queen took on the responsibilities of the Crown at home that two of her subjects, Archibald and Caroline Chisholm, serving in the outposts of what was to come to be called her Empire, embarked on the ship the *Emerald Isle* to Australia. The date was March 24th 1838.

**Notes**

1. *Caroline Chisholm, The Emigrant's Friend*, by G. Elliot Anstruther, Catholic Trust Society, London 1917.
2. *Memoirs of Mrs Caroline Chisholm*, by Eneas Mackenzie, London 1852.
3. *India Register*, 1837 'compiled, by Permission of the East-India Company, from the *Official returns received at the East India House* by F. Clark, of the Secretary's Office, East-India House.'

# Chapter Five

# Australia

The journey from India to Australia was long and demanding. The *Emerald Isle* was a sound ship, adequately comfortable by the standards of the day but still offering only cramped quarters for her passengers. The Chisholm family group comprised Caroline and Archibald with the two little boys, plus three Indian servants. These would help the family on the voyage and then return in due course to India, taking their earnings back to their families there.

At Mauritius the passengers disembarked. There was to be a month's delay while repairs to the ship were carried out. Caroline and Archibald were certainly being given plenty of time to think about the wisdom of the trip to Australia. Their spirits were high and everything seemed new and exciting. Army life gradually receded from their minds and conversations. The little boys grew familiar first with the routine of ship life and then with the scents and sounds of exotic Mauritius. When the passengers were finally on board again for the last stage of the journey all hopes and thoughts turned to Australia.

In going to this great island continent, they were venturing on territory that had within living memory been regarded as virtually beyond the limits of the known world. Back in England, there were few people who had been to Australia and returned to talk about it. It was known only as a terrible place of exile for banished criminals, bereft of most civilised comforts and home to the strangest of wild animals and birds. Because it lay in the Southern hemisphere, its seasons were reversed, and the months of November, December, and January had scorching heat while July and August were cooler.

Yet it was also a place of excitement, exploration, and fascination. Explorers were still mapping out its coasts and trying to discover more about its vast interior. Books were being written about its kangaroos and kookaburras, its duck-billed platypus and koala bear, its stunning scenery and venomous snakes. As the *Emerald Isle*, buffeted by the seas, ploughed its way steadily towards Australia, Caroline and Archibald mingled a sense of adventure with a mood of apprehension and concern about just what awaited them there.

Australia's first contacts with the modern world are still a matter of debate. It seems that the first person from Europe to sight the southern continental land-mass was the Dutch explorer William Janszoon in 1605. For about ten years after 1616 Dutch navigators saw much of the west coast, and then in 1643 Abel Tasman discovered an island off the main land-mass, and this he named Van Dieman's Land, after Anthony van Dieman, the Dutch governor-general of Holland's territories in the East Indies, who had sponsored his expedition. Eventually, some 200 years later, this island was to bear his own name and be called Tasmania, and the water separating it from the mainland the Tasman Sea.

Significant European settlement in Australia only began with Captain Cook's expedition in the 1780s, usually described as the first official 'discovery' of the territory. As is well known, the land was used for a long period chiefly as a British penal settlement. The American colonies could no longer be used for this purpose, having fought and won a war for full independence from the British Crown. William Pitt, the Prime Minister, announced in the House of Commons that transportation to Australia offered the cheapest way of reducing Britain's prison population, thus solving the problem of chronic overcrowding in the country's gaols. On May 13th 1787 the first fleet of eleven ships sailed from England with approximately 1,030 people on board, of whom about 760 were convicts, under the command of Captain Arthur Phillips, who was to become the first Governor of the new colony. The voyage lasted three months. The fleet reached Botany Bay on January 18th 1788. The land there was found unsuitable for permanent settlement, so the ships sailed further along the coast. Here lay a great natural harbour, extraordinary in its width and beauty. The party landed on January 26th – a date honoured by subsequent generations of Australians as Australia Day – and founded a settlement. The town they were creating was formally named Sydney, after Lord Sydney, Secretary of State for the Colonies.

To later generations, it seems bizarre as well as callous that a nation should have sent its petty criminals on a long and dangerous journey to the other side of the world, there to suffer harsh punishment under savage and brutal conditions with little likelihood of ever seeing their families again. What scope did such a system offer for repentance or renewal of life? How could it be squared with any tradition of mercy?

Yet it did create the beginnings of a settlement in this territory, and out of those first convicts and those who guarded them came a community which, for all its brutality and harshness, succeeded in taming large areas of land and producing food and shelter of sorts out of it.

Caroline and Archibald's first glimpses of Australia were not of the convict territory in New South Wales, however, but of the port of Adelaide, much further south. This township had been named after Queen Adelaide, the wife of King William IV. It was a small and struggling community – but it spelt security and safety to the passengers who had spent many weeks at sea and were glad to be on dry land. The Chisholms did not plan to settle here – they were heading for Sydney, the major port.

How good it was to feel solid land beneath the feet again after the perpetual motion of the ship! How delicious to eat fresh food, to sleep in a proper bed – albeit in the humble accommodation that was all the port offered by way of an inn for travellers – and to be able to get clothes washed. The family revelled in the comfort of it all, and recovered from the smells and memories of the sea voyage. They found that the settlers here were friendly people, eager to talk to newcomers, to gain news and to give information. The arrival of a ship was always a big event and every group of passengers was pumped for news. In return the settlers spoke about their lives – their hopes and plans, the prices they were getting for crops or sheep, the steady growth of the town and its port, and their worries about the future. Many hopes were being invested here. Adelaide had been conceived as a settlement that was to have no convict labour — everyone who arrived came voluntarily as a free settler. The Chisholms did not stay long enough to learn everything about Australian life and lore, but they picked up a lot and they liked what they learned.

Then it was time to get back on board again for the trip to Sydney — but this would be a further longish voyage as the *Emerald Isle* was going first to Hobart Town on Van Dieman's Land. The ship sailed out across the Tasman Sea and the passengers would have three weeks on the island settlement before embarking on the final leg of the journey to New South Wales.

Hobart was another friendly settlement. It offered more bustle and life than Adelaide, and exuded a greater air of prosperity and success. Its history was longer — Adelaide had only been settled a few years previously — and among the residents were many old hands. There was a great deal to learn and talk about.

Finally, they were on their way to Sydney. They had been told about is magnificent natural harbour, but even so its size and splendour took their breath away at first. The water glittered blue and clear, gulls screeched and the busy quayside teemed with life. Here was no small outpost but a thriving port, one that was proud of itself and assertive in its attitude to newcomers. Crowds had gathered to greet the arrival of the ship, and there were shouts and cries as carriers hurried forward to offer their services with the luggage, and passengers were greeted.

As at Adelaide and Hobart, Archibald arranged for accommodation in the town and the family moved into an hotel. Caroline wanted to see everything, and take in all she could of this place that was to be her new home.

New South Wales was a mixed society. Convicts were still there in substantial numbers, locked up in gaols or working as forced labour along the roads or on the farms. Some had gone on to become 'ticket of leave' men who were allowed to acquire land and farms of their own or to work and thus eventually earn their passage home. Many more had died in misery and were buried in the prison cemeteries around Sydney.

The convicts had been joined, however, by quite a number of free settlers – men who had gone out to try their luck in the new and raw colony. Some farmed, some were traders, some worked on the roads or at various jobs in the port. Then there were successful farmers who had arrived with sufficient money to buy a good plot of land and were already making comfortable lives for themselves. Often, these were the younger sons of prosperous families in Britain. The oldest son in the family had inherited the family home, and the younger ones were left with a choice of an Army career, the Church, or the Colonies. Those who opted for the Colonies brought with them a spirit of enthusiasm and adventure. They felt that England was too small a place to accommodate all that they wanted to do, and that Australia's wide lands offered opportunities unknown at home.

Then there was also a substantial community associated with the government administration of the colony – the Governor himself, of course, and his staff, but also the Army with all its usual formidable trimmings of barracks and bustle.

This was New South Wales – so named by the earliest settlers because it reminded them of the countryside of that part of Britain. It included the territory around Port Phillip Bay (named after Captain Arthur Phillip) which was later to be known as the state of Victoria.

An Australian history sums up the position 'About 157,000 convicts were transported to Australia between 1788 and 1868. Of these, under the system in force up to 1840, 80,000 were sent to New South Wales (including a few working in the Port Phillip and Moreton Bay districts which were then part of the colony) and 32,000 to Van Dieman's Land'[1]. The government gave no assistance to a convict who had served his sentence and wanted to return home – he had to work to raise his fare, or rely on the charity of others.

The Chisholms came with enough money to pay for accommodation until they could find a house to rent, and their two small boys – freed from the constraints of the ship – must have relished the change of scene.

It did not take long for the family to settle into the small colony. Their Army connections brought them an immediate acceptance in the community. The climate, although warm, seemed to lack India's oppressive heat. Sydney had the appearance of a town that knew it had a future. There was talk of the immense possibilities of acquiring land further into 'the bush' and of the fortunes that might be made from farming. Already, some were becoming rich. The plight of the convicts was much discussed. They were viewed with pity rather than contempt. There was embarrassment that they brought down the tone of the colony, and much pressure for the whole transportation system to end. Families who were settling with a view to acquiring land and passing it on to their children looked askance at the fighting and drunkenness that was known to be part of life in the more sordid areas of the docks. There was a desire, especially among the ladies, to establish a sense of order and gentility. Mrs Chisholm, fresh from India, would have attracted attention as someone worth cultivating, with experience of the world outside Australia.

Gradually, as they made contacts and established themselves, Caroline and Archibald found themselves part of the community. There was a willingness to help, and a certain cheeriness and friendship which Caroline decided was unique to Australia – people were unpretentious and there was much less formality in social relations than there was back in England. It was also very different from the Army community in India.

It was not difficult to practise the Catholic faith in this new colony. There had been provision, of sorts, for Catholic convicts for some while and now there was a formalised Church structure establishing churches wherever possible. Back in February 1833 Father William Ullathorne – later to be a notable bishop – had arrived in Australia and reported back to his superiors that it should be split off from Mauritius (with which it was then linked as a missionary territory) and treated as an autonomous ecclesiastical district. On 13th September 1835 Bishop J.B. Polding had arrived as Vicar Apostolic for New Holland. On 29th July 1836 the Governor of the Colony, Governor Bourke, passed the Church Act, allowing all religious bodies to be established on an equal footing. This was in line with the new thinking that had developed back in Britain following Catholic Emancipation.

In 1841 Bishop Polding was reporting that he had in his diocese 40,000 Catholics, attended by 24 priests. There were also some nuns — Sisters of Charity — and in addition to several small chapels there were 15 actual churches, and a total of 31 Catholic schools.

For Captain and Mrs Chisholm, then, it was perfectly acceptable to be seen going to the Catholic church, and to be recognised as belonging to that faith.

There was a sense of times changing in New South Wales. Everyone knew that the convict era must be drawing to its close. Successive governors of the territory had made grants of land to anyone who was willing to feed, clothe, and employ convict labour. The owners of land thus included ex-convicts, free settlers, and officers of the garrisons. The work of Captain John Macarthur at the end of the previous century, in developing sheep farming, had given Australia what was to be her greatest source of wealth. The merino sheep, a Spanish breed imported from South Africa, was proving hugely successful and the wool industry was growing.

Emigration from Britain and settlement in the colonies was beginning to be seen as a great hope for the future. Back in Britain Mr Patrick Matthew had just published *Emigration Fields: North America, The Cape, Australia and New Zealand*, a handbook 'describing these countries, and giving a comparative view of the advantages they present to British settlers.'[2] He was not too enthusiastic about Australia, saying that the climate was too dry, with a danger of droughts. The bark hung off the trees in an unsightly way! The grass grew thinly and cattle dung dried before it could be used as good manure. On the other hand, the land was good for sheep-rearing as there was no hard winter requiring the harvesting and storage of hay. He had some interesting comments on the appearance of the British: 'Those born in the country — the Australian British — are generally of a good tall size, to which the plenty of animal food will no doubt conduce. But notwithstanding of salubrity, the infirmities of age and wrinkles appear sooner than in Britain, the teeth also ... decay at a very early period, which would augur some deficiency in the digestive functions ... As in all new countries, even though a little warmer than the parent country, light-coloured hair is more frequent than in the parent country, the complexion is also inclining to be a brick-red cast, without the rose-bloom cheek.'

But there were big social problems ahead. Mr Matthew bemoaned the great disparity between the sexes in the colony. There was a very low birth-rate among the settlers, simply because so few of them could find wives — there were not enough females coming out from Britain! 'Perhaps no colony in the world has been so absurdly conducted as New South Wales. It is not long since the proportion of males to females was ten to one, while there was a still greater disparity between the grown-ups of both sexes.' His solution was that soldiers garrisoned in Australia should be allowed to bring out their wives — this would mean that some children would be born in the colony. He did not think that the same privilege might be extended to the convicts, of whom he wrote in crude and insulting terms, evidently seeing them as being of no importance and deserving of little attention or pity.

Once the Chisholms were settled in a pleasant house on the outskirts of Sydney, Caroline became uncomfortably aware of the seamier side of the colony's life. Around the port area, especially at night, there gathered the people who were the unfortunate reminders of a sad underworld. Here were the ex-convicts — some still bearing the marks of hideous floggings on their back — down on their luck and without hope of a passage home. Here were newly-arrived emigrants who had found no work or lodgings, or who had been robbed of the savings and possessions with which they had hoped to start new lives. Here — perhaps the most pitiful group of all — were young women who had travelled out from Britain on their own, hoping to escape from the workhouse or from the bitter poverty of an orphan's life in a grim city. They had no jobs awaiting them — they were not wanted for casual labour on road-building or unloading ships and could not find transport out to the bush areas to seek out farms where they might find shelter. Too often, their best chance of survival lay in various forms of prostitution — finding a male 'protector' who would offer food and shelter or ending up in a brothel under the vicious direction of a woman who had appeared to offer friendship and 'regular work'.

Sometimes the brothel madams even went straight to a ship's side when it appeared in the port, taking the girls as soon as they arrived. Later, alone and abandoned and perhaps expecting a child, a girl would live as an outcast on the city's fringes, sleeping rough where she could and contemplating a future of hunger and misery leading to an early death.

Perhaps this was the sort of situation that Mr Matthew had in mind when he wrote scathingly 'New South Wales being a penal settlement with nearly one-half of the grown-up population consisting of convicts, moral feeling and the tone of society must in some measure be affected. In the business of common life there, it is said, every man proceeds as if no other principle but selfishness of the most gross character regulated the actions of his neighbours. But it would have been folly to expect that the morals of the inmates of a prison-house, containing such an immense number of criminals, could have been better than they really are.'[3]

Caroline, however, with her knowledge and experience gained from her work in India, had an entirely different and more humane outlook. Had she not learned that the little girls whom many had dismissed as common soldiers' children, unworthy of any education or training, had proved eager and enthusiastic pupils in a bright and happy school? Offered accomodation, friendship, and a way out of their difficulties, most human beings were likely to prove to possess qualities that had not surfaced before. Among the rough colonists, and the penniless women reduced to street life, there were surely many who only needed a little practical support to enable them to find a challenging alternative.

Already, Archibald had given practical support to some of his fellow countrymen. Meeting a forlorn group of Highlanders one day in Sydney, he had joined in their conversation — they spoke only Gaelic and were finding it impossible to find themselves accommodation or jobs. With Caroline's support, he lent them a little money and discussed their problems with them. But it was her advice that proved the most valuable: why not spend their money on ropes and other equipment and get jobs as woodcutters? Everyone always wanted firewood for cooking and there would probably be a good trade if they travelled from door to door offering supplies. Not long afterwards, the Chisholms met them again, busy and successful. Exchanging greetings and swapping news was immensely satisfying. In this new colony, sometimes all that newcomers needed was a bit of advice or information from someone who was prepared to offer genuine friendly assistance.

Any attempts at philanthropy on Caroline's part, however, had to wait. A new baby was now expected. He was born on 30th July 1839, a third boy, whom they named Henry. With his brothers Archie and William this made a full and happy household. Caroline needed help, and found a most able and competent assistant with the children in a Miss Galvin, who became a firm friend and was to remain with the family for many years.

New South Wales was a far more attractive place than Madras in which to raise a family, and as she watched the children playing in the sunshine, with the new baby gurgling in his cradle on the cool verandah, Caroline felt the wisdom of the decision to come to this new colony. The little boys revelled in the life here. It was a rural childhood bringing many of the blessings and pleasures that she had known growing up in Northamptonshire. There was plenty of space and fresh air, a closeness to the world of nature, and an ample supply of good fresh food. There were friends with a shared sense of commitment to the life of the neighbourhood, and the pleasure of celebrating its festivals and anniversaries. There was plenty of hospitality and social activity – neighbourly suppers and gatherings to welcome newcomers or to honour Christmas, New Year, Easter, or a good harvest.

The boys' fair skins needed to be protected from the sun by wide-brimmed hats – but these were common wear among all the settlers. They needed to learn the country lore of the area – to be watchful for snakes (although these tended to stay well clear of busy houses and gardens), and respectful of the dangers of the heat. They had learned quickly, and already could remember no home but this one. India belonged to a remote world.

Letters home to England took months to arrive. Caroline wrote regularly, telling her mother about the new baby and giving reassurances of her own health and happiness. She knew that these letters would be passed around, read aloud and savoured, as were those she received back from her mother. She tried to tell her boys about their grandmother in England, and to give them some flavour of life there. It all seemed very distant to them, and like many colonial children they lived with a vague impression of a far-away place of an almost mythical character, inhabited by a Queen and regularly drenched by rain and snow. Letters and their mother's tales of her childhood were the only link with that world, and belonged to quiet evenings after family prayers, and would always be associated with their mother's nostalgia and those treasured letters. The arrival of a ship from Britain at Sydney harbour brought a flurry of excitement when it was known that it carried mail, and for a long while afterwards neighbours would share news and discuss things together.

A visit into Sydney was quite an expedition from the Chisholms' home on the outskirts of the town. It made a busy day out, and Caroline would usually combine some shopping with a visit to friends. While news was exchanged and refreshments enjoyed, there was also an opportunity to see how the town was changing and what new buildings were going up or other developments were taking place. On town trips, Archibald also liked to buy a newspaper and to catch up on the controversies of the day. A walk around the port was also always exciting, especially for the small boys.

It was on one such visit that Caroline came across a forlorn group of girls, sitting together in the harbour, looking miserable, dirty, and hungry. It was impossible to pass by without making some enquiry about them. Caroline approached and asked them what was wrong. They turned out to be new arrivals from Britain, still ill from the horrors of the journey, and with nowhere to go and practically no money between them.

They were 'Bounty' migrants, shipped from Britain under the system through which ships' captains received money for the number of settlers they could bring. There had been pressure to bring out more single females, and so shiploads were now beginning to arrive. A harsh reality awaited these emigrants. There was no recognised job agency, and no accommodation on offer to those without funds. Many of the girls were no more than children, not yet out of their teens. Most of them could not read or write. Their journey had been horrific − crammed together in filthy and smelly conditions, sometimes terrorised by members of the crew who knew them to be improverished and without the protection of family or friends. They had seen death and disease on the journey, and now that they had finally arrived, it was only to find themselves completely abandoned while more fortunate passengers settled into hotels or lodgings. These girls desperately needed some basic security and assistance. Inevitably, Caroline ended up doing what her heart dictated − she took some of the most pitiful into her own home.

If she had believed half the stories told to her by long-time settlers she would have expected the girls to steal, cheat, lie, or turn the house into a brothel overnight. But none of this happened. Instead, the girls proved grateful for a chance to wash themselves and their clothes, to eat a decent meal, and to sleep in decent beds. Caroline made enquiries among her friends and acquaintances, and soon found that there was considerable demand for them in local families. There were plenty of jobs on offer. A colonial home needed all the help it could find, for cooking and cleaning and household tasks, laundry-work and helping a new mother with a baby. The girls themselves were only too anxious to work hard and prove themselves in return for good lodgings and modest wages. In no time, these Chisholm family visitors were setting off, their few belongings washed and re-packed, to new homes. Caroline was shortly to have the satisfaction of hearing that they had settled well, and even started a fashion locally, with other families seeking more like them. Suddenly, an emigrant girl newly-arrived from England or Ireland seemed to be an asset to a harassed housewife in the colony, rather than a problem to avoid.

Things then moved more quickly than Caroline could ever have imagined. The word spread rapidly that Mrs Chisholm was the person to contact if you were a settled family wanting a servant, or a girl down on her luck and sleeping rough in 'The Rocks'. She was stopped in the street when walking out with Miss Galvin and the boys, and tired travellers knocked at her door, enquiring if she was the lady who offered help. Clearly, she was going to have to organise herself.

Ideas and plans began to co-ordinate themselves in her head: why not bring together some of the people who might be prepared to offer structured and practical help to the newly-arrived girls? Should not the Governor be involved in what was happening? How about a proper establishment – a Home for Emigrant Girls? Surely funds could be raised for this? Archibald, who had supported her whole-heartedly in her projects in India, was enthusiastic about her plans. He knew all about her formidable skills of organisation, and had seen her rise to the challenge of creating the school in Madras, overcoming numerous difficulties and prejudices along the way.

It was partly her own sense of happiness and well-being that prompted Caroline to be so concerned about the plight of other, less fortunate women. Her own long journey to India as an Army bride had ended in Archibald's loving welcome, with a home ready and waiting and a happy future stretching ahead. How very different was the plight of these girls who, like her, set off from Britain on a long sea journey but, unlike her, faced only misery, disappointment and homelessness at the end of it.

The speed of the development of Caroline's efforts, however, took both her and Archibald by surprise. Indeed, Caroline was frightened by it. She was a nobody in the colony. Settled for not much over a year, she appeared to be embarking on schemes that ought to have been the task of those who had been active in the colony for far longer, or who held public office there. Her husband was not on the Governor's staff, nor were they rich or influential. There was a grave danger of her becoming a laughing-stock, a well-meaning newcomer who was going to be taken advantage of by the very people she sought to serve.

Nevertheless, she persevered, and found that there was enthusiastic support for what she was doing and much goodwill among the colonists. The practical results were also immensely satisfying.

However her own family life also claimed her attention. Archibald's leave from the Army was ending, and he would have to return to India. In January 1840, at the height of the Australian summer, he must sail back to Madras. For some time they had been discussing the future.

The children were flourishing in Australia. The family had made many friends and had created a comfortable and settled home in the colony. India was a notoriously dangerous place for a young baby. After much debate they took the difficult decision that Archibald should return to India alone. He already knew that he did not seek to prolong his Army career. As soon as his duty was over, he would return to Australia, and together they would start on the next stage of their lives. Perhaps, if all went well, they would go back home to England.

Caroline knew that this was a wise decision and once they had made it she faced the future calmly. Archibald must not have undue worries about his young family as he departed to fulfil the final part of his Army duty. She would take care of the family until his return – and then they would have the joy of returning home to England, and renewing links with her mother who would see her grandchildren for the first time.

Archibald was glad that Caroline would have work to do in the period when they would be separated. He told her that he foresaw the care of emigrants, and indeed the whole question of emigration, would be her special field.

Parting would be difficult. The children would be much older and taller when they next saw their father. Caroline also knew of the dangers of a soldier's life: if war loomed in India anything could happen. She tried to face things realistically and to be calm and cheerful, accepting the fact of being an Army wife. She was not one to complain, whatever befell them all.

As 1839 ended they had a final family Christmas together. There was Mass in Melbourne's Catholic church, and then exchanges of greetings with friends in the warm summer sunshine while the children played excitedly. Inevitably, everybody contrasted the scene with Christmases back in England or Ireland amid rain, snow, or sleet. Then there was a full traditional Christmas dinner – no concession made to the difference in climate as roasted meat and hot vegetables were brought steaming from the oven to the table. There were gifts to exchange and the fun of sharing the children's pleasure in their new toys − and an evening of nostaligia as past family Christmases were recalled, old songs sung, friends and relatives remembered.

It all made the separation just a short while later much harder. As January opened, Caroline helped supervise Archibald's packing, checking and re-checking to ensure that he would have everything that could make both the long sea voyage and then life in India as bearable as possible.

Yet, this was far harder than the initial separation long ago in Brighton. Now Archibald was leaving the comforts of a very happy family life, to go back to an Army life with which he was all too familiar. His children would change and grow, his baby son would be running about and talking when he returned and would greet him as a stranger.

He faced not only the discomfort of a long sea journey but also the knowledge that it was only the prelude to a lengthy separation which neither he nor his wife had any power to shorten. Throughout her life, Caroline would always have a special feeling for families who had to endure enforced separation and the fears of the dangers and hardships of long sea journeys. She knew all about it − the tears at parting, the repeated reassurances, the hugs and embraces and cherished farewell messages, and then the weeks of waiting for letters and the worry over rumours of shipwrecks or storms at sea. She also felt for the divided families − the children who missed their father and the wives who waited and worried. Archibald arrived back in India on 27th March and returned to Army duty. Letters back and forth between him and Caroline were to be their only links for the next four long years. As Caroline came to terms with life without her husband, she was determined to use the time creatively, concentrating her efforts on helping people who needed her, and following Archibald's own advice about using her talents and skills to assist newcomers to the colony.

**Notes**

1. *The Australian Encyclopedia*, published by the Grolier Society of Australia, undated.

2. *Emigration Fields. North America, The Cape, Australia and New Zealand, describing these countries, and giving a comparative view of the advantages they present to British settlers* by Patrick Matthew, Adam and Charles Black, Edinburgh, Longmans, London, 1839.
3. op cit.

# Chapter Six

# Something Ventured

In the middle of Sydney, not far from the busy docks area stood the old Immigration Barracks. This was a forbidding building, owned by the colonial authorities but now disused. It had been a centre for the Government-sponsored emigrants who arrived before the Bounty Scheme was introduced. Now it was abandoned and rat-infested, with the exception of a small area used for stores. Nearby, the Bounty migrants camped while making their own plans for the future. They were given rations and they lit their own fires to make tea and cook their meat and 'damper' (flour and water paste, cooked over an open fire on the end of a stick to make a sort of bread roll).

Caroline, alone now that Archibald had gone, was trying to grapple seriously with the task of giving some practical help to the newly-arrived immigrants, but the task seemed enormous. Her own family responsibilities were already quite substantial – did it really make any sense at all to be trying to take on the task of caring for complete strangers?

She was beginning to learn from the girls she had befriended just how savage their experiences on board ship had been. The cramped and filthy quarters, with no proper sanitation or personal privacy, had meant that they had lost their sense of self-respect. They had been surrounded by coarse language, vulgarity and crude jokes, and had become hardened in their own defence. If she wanted to give them any help at all here in Australia, she would have to introduce a whole new note of hope and optimism into their lives. Their sensitivity had been destroyed. Theirs had been a fight for sheer survival.

Caroline recognised that this was to be a struggle for the moral high ground. She must enlist the help of people whose consciences she could touch, who would share a sense of outrage at the way in which their fellow human beings had been treated and a desire to help them reclaim themselves.

When she went into Sydney to look over the possible options for starting a practical project, she realised that if she were to open a home for migrant girls, the old barracks would be the obvious place. But it would have to be turned into something quite different – a place of hope and optimism, clean and attractive. Here, girls would have to feel that they were truly safe. They would have to relearn the decencies of normal life – keeping themselves and their clothes clean, establishing co-operation and friendship, making plans for the future. It must also have proper office space where business could be carried out in an atmosphere of confidence and efficiency, where prospective employers could come to interview candidates, and where records could be kept of wages and job specifications.

Yet, nothing happened immediately. For some months Caroline continued to work as she had been doing, as an unofficial information bureau, finding work for people as and where she could. She acted in a way that was natural to her, not out of any financial motive or as some kind of busybody, and people seemed instinctively to recognise this and respond accordingly. Her reputation grew as a reliable source of information and of help and protection for those who needed it.

Caroline recognised that the work she was doing was needed on a massive scale. Previously she had not fully appreciated how serious the situation was. Large numbers of young women were being forced into evil and degrading lifestyles through no fault of their own. Both from a practical, social and spiritual point of view this represented something profoundly tragic.

It seemed clear to Caroline that what was required was a properly organised project, a centre where newcomers could be welcomed and an employment agency administered. It was not enough just to express pious hopes that the authorities would produce a solution, and it was quite unacceptable to lift up respectable hands in horror and speak smugly about the immorality of the 'lower classes of migrant.' Caroline also knew that she had the necessary skills to do this job and knowledge of the problems involved. She knew that her work in India had taught her how to finance, run and organise such an institution. But she hesitated at the thought of such an enormous undertaking, although the more she hesitated, the more her conscience troubled her.

Knowing what she now did of the lives these girls were living, could she safely wrap herself up in her own family life and ignore the problem? How would God view her actions if she did? Would she be conniving in the sin if she did not face up to the necessary work? She was later to write about this: 'About this time, several young women whom I had served, advised others to write to me: I did all I could to aid them in their prospects by advice, or recommending them to situations; but the number increased, and I saw that my plan, if carried into effect, would serve *all*. My delay pressed on my mind as a sin; and when I heard of a poor girl suffering distress and losing her reputation in consequence, I felt I was not clear of her sin, for I did not do all I could to prevent it.'

This was the voice of conscience, and not merely a desire to be busy about a new project for its own sake. For the committed Catholic, conscience was a serious issue. By now it was a new year, 1841. In England, spring was coming. Here, with the reversed seasons, it was the beginning of a much welcomed Autumn. Lent came in with cooling breezes and a refreshing break from the incessant sun. It was a time for penance and repentance, for begging forgiveness from God and beginning again in newness of life. Caroline was teaching her own small boys about Lent and Easter, but above all she must apply it to her own life.

The liturgical life of the Catholic Church functioned here as around the globe. Perhaps it had a special meaning here in this raw colony, where the great drama of good and evil was being played out so clearly in the lives of men and women wrenched from the lands where their ancestors had lived for generations. Caroline knelt among the other penitents in the small Catholic church for confession, attended Mass on the Lenten Sundays, prayed and meditated at home, took part in the solemn liturgy for Good Friday. All the time, she was aware that God was posing a challenging series of questions to her about her own life and the direction it was taking.

'During Lent and Easter of that year I suffered much', she was to recall later. 'But on the Easter Sunday, I was enabled, at the altar of our Lord, to make an offering of my talents to the God Who gave them. I promised to know neither country nor creed, but to try to serve all justly and impartially. I asked only to be enabled to keep these poor girls from being tempted, by their need, to mortal sin; and resolved that to accomplish this, I would in every way sacrifice my feelings — surrender all comfort — nor in fact consider my own wishes or feelings but wholly devote myself to the work I had in hand. I felt my offering was accepted and God's blessing was on my work: but it was His will to permit may serious difficulties to be thrown in my way, and to conduct me through a rugged path of deep humiliation.'[1]

The commitment she had made had perhaps something of the same quality as John Wesley's dramatic moment of conversion in London before he devoted his life to preaching what was to become known as Methodism, or General Booth's giving of his full allegiance to divine purposes in founding the Salvation Army. Her subsequent work was not to be notably religious, but its spiritual foundation was in fact central to it. From this time on, she felt at peace about what she was doing. With an attitude of service and a sense of trying to be faithful to what she had promised God and felt Him accept, she now went ahead in faith.

Her first decision was to write to the Governor of the Colony, Sir George Gipps. It was a decision that took some courage. Caroline was embarking on a course of action that might bring her considerable financial risks, and much embarrassment and humiliation. Sir George already knew about her informal work, but had never met her. Caroline's letter introduced the subject of the plight of destitute new arrivals to the colony, and begged for the use of the old Immigrants Barracks as a home for girls. It was to be the forerunner of many, many letters that she was to write over the years ahead to those in public authority — pleading, enquiring, setting out a case, arguing a point of view, asking for practical assistance.

The letter that arrived at the Governor's mansion was probably not entirely welcome. Mrs Chisholm was becoming quite well known for her work, and was acquiring the reputation of a moral guardian. Perhaps Sir George thought that she would come and preach him a sermon if he answered her request for an interview. He might also have felt that if she attempted to do so, he could probably brush her off politely with a few well-chosen phrases which would make them both feel comfortable. Whatever his thoughts, he replied with a formal invitation for Caroline to visit him. He was later to confess that he 'expected to have seen an old lady in cap and spectacles who would have talked to me about my soul. I was amazed when my aide introduced me to a handsome, stately young woman who proceeded to reason the question as though she thought her reason and experience to be worth as much as mine.'[2]

Sir George found himself both impressed and disconcerted. Here was a lady of common sense and considerable charm, much younger than he had imagined and with a sense of confidence and determination. Although he maintained his opposition to the use of the old barracks as a home for girls, he felt his position to be a weak one. If Mrs Chisholm succeeded in proving herself a capable organiser and if she brought together others prepared to help in the scheme, he might have to change his mind. That, at any rate, was what Caroline decided after meeting him. They parted on friendly if cautious terms. She settled down to work. She must take some more specific plans, perhaps with the aid of a committee established for the purpose. This she now set about doing, writing from an address in Jamison Street, and trying to interest any people of influence that she could, especially the ladies. She had a strong sense that in the end official help would be forthcoming. This was confirmed when Lady Gipps herself agreed to head the committee. The Sydney newspapers also proved helpful, by running a story about the plight of the destitute girls. One was found wandering around in a state of such confusion that she was thought to be drunk, and punished with an hour in the stocks — only after she was released was it realised that she had simply been fainting from complete lack of food. She had not eaten for several days.

Eventually, the evident genuine concern of the ladies on the committee, and the quiet persistent strength of Mrs Chisholm, produced the result. The immigration barracks were handed over. There was, however, a catch. Caroline was asked by Sir George to sign a statement agreeing that her work should not require the use of any official funds. The message was clear: she could not expect Government money to rescue her if things went wrong. Initially, this did not seem to her to be a huge problem. Her committee was at work, and several people had pledged money and support. She had also received encouragement from the clergy, both Catholic and Protestant. But she had reckoned without the 'serious difficulties and humiliations' that were to come her way.

Suddenly, with the immediate prospect of hard work and dedication looming before them, people who had offered help started to backtrack. Promised money was not forthcoming. Clergymen suddenly announced that the scheme was foolish. Perhaps some of the Catholic community felt that a public failure on the part of one prominent Catholic would taint them all. Perhaps others felt that her concept of a Home which would be of service to the whole community and not to just one religious group was in some way dangerous. This was not a period of ecumenism. Sectarianism was rife in Sydney, and provided much spice to life. People's faith was strongly linked to their own sense of cultural identity. Caroline, English and Catholic, was rather unusual. The Irish clergy were sometimes wary of her, and this communicated itself rapidly to their parishioners. Among certain Protestants, she was already acquiring an aura of being a tool of sinister Roman plotting, an innocent dupe of clergy bent on the destruction of the Protestant cause throughout the British Empire.

Caroline's spirits started to sag, and then finally slipped down into despair. She felt alone and very vulnerable. She had brought her name — and Archibald's — into the public arena, and would in all probability now see it humiliated. There was no one on whom she could lean for comfort and reassurance. Had she done completely the wrong thing in attempting to take on a vast new project? It all became so difficult that she finally decided to leave Sydney and go to stay for a few days in Parramatta while she quietly thought things over. She wanted to be away from the pressures and the gossip about her plans. Perhaps a time of peaceful contemplation would show her the way ahead.

The harbour was bathed in evening sunlight as she walked along the shore, deep in her thoughts, a covered basket containing an overnight change of clothes on her arm. The children were safe with Miss Galvin for a few days. She felt that she should spend the time in quiet thought and prayer, seeking guidance. Friends in Parramatta would put her up — they lived not far from where the ferry across the river would set her off. She walked slowly and purposefully, thinking over and over again about her letter to the Governor — had it been wise? — and about the members of her committee — did any have any special grudge or had she been accidentally rude or hurtful to any of them?

As she drew near the harbour she realised that she had been dawdling. She was in danger of missing the ferry. She gathered speed and hurried on. Her bonnet slipped back as she tried to run, and the basket seemed heavier. She changed it from hand to hand in an effort to lighten it. As she rounded the corner from where she could view the ferry crossing, she saw the heavy steamer gently slip its moorings and head out into the river. She had missed it. This seemed the final blow. An added twist was that earlier on in her walk, she had been stopped by some friends who were also on their way to the steamer, in a pony and trap, and who offered her a lift. She had told them that she was enjoying her walk and wanted to be alone for a while. Now they would be aboard, looking for her and remarking on her absence.

It was much too far to go back home, and she was stranded. The only possibility was to stay with friends — and she had in fact earlier been invited to a small social gathering that evening at a house not far away. She had given a vague promise that, if she happened to be in town, she would attend — but had then decided on the Parramatta trip. Now she must think again, and accept the invitation and its offer of overnight accommodation. She tidied her hair and bonnet, picked up her basket again, and set off towards the town centre.

She was depressed. At the party, there would inevitably be talk of her project, and she would have to appear bright and cheerful, dedicated to overcoming all obstacles and confident that the plan was a good one. She did not in the least feel up to it. A sense of lethargy almost overcame her. If only Archie were there at her arm, and they could just go somewhere and talk!

As she drew nearer to the centre of town, near Perry's Hotel, a girl hurried suddenly past her from a side-street. Their eyes met for a brief moment, and Caroline instantly recognised her. It was Flora − a lovely Scottish girl from the Highlands whom she had befriended weeks before. They had parted in embarrassment − impatient at attempts to find her a job, Flora had become friendly with a man who was clearly not offering marriage but merely an 'arrangement', and against Caroline's advice she had gone off with him. She had been seen subsequently in smart clothes and spending freely in the local shops. She had carefully avoided Caroline although she had flaunted her new wealth and apparrent success in front of some of the other girls, some of whom had been temporarily impressed.

How tragically different she looked now. Flora's complexion showed all too clearly that she had been drinking, and as she brushed past Caroline there was a strong smell of rum. Her appearance was dishevelled and she seemed to have been weeping heavily. She did not pause but hurried down the street, looking back only once and then quickening her pace. Caroline had a sudden swift sickening feeling that the girl was going to kill herself. She hurried forward, determined to overtake her, and caught up with her by the bridge. 'Where are you going?' Caroline panted out, and received only the distraught answer 'To hell!' Flora attempted to get away, but Caroline put her hand gently on her arm and asked her what was wrong. At first the girl said she was on her way to a house where she now worked, but when Caroline said she would walk with her she stopped and sat down on a nearby bench, refusing to go any further. She was silent in the face of further questioning, gazing only at the water. Then she broke down in tears.

Caroline hesitated to ask the question uppermost in her mind. She put it delicately 'Are you −' she hesitated 'Are you a mother?' Flora clasped her hand and shook her head. No, she was not. But she was desperate and abandoned. Her male friend had left her − without any word or warning − and gone off with another girl. She was penniless and friendless, regarded by others as being no better than a prostitute. Her one thought that evening had been to go to the place where he had taken her for evening walks, near Lavenders Ferry, and fling herself into the water there.

They sat for a long while, talking as the story came out. Dusk was falling as Caroline led her back towards the town and found a family who had helped with accommodation on previous occasions and were willing to offer a bed for the night to someone in trouble. In the morning, Caroline promised, she would be back and together they would work something out for the future.

Drained and exhausted, Caroline then finally turned her steps back towards her own destination and the social conviviality that awaited her. Tired as she was, however, something had been sparked inside her — from now on, fear had left her. She could not possibly let girls like Flora down. No matter what the opposition or difficulties, she would somehow go ahead with her campaign, and get the Immigration Barracks turned into a proper Home, so that all would have somewhere to go. From now on, no opposition could wear her down and no amount of sectarian strife or insults about her religion or motivation would deter her.

At the party that evening she held her own against intrusive questions, snide comments or general enquiries concerning her work. Yes, she replied confidently to all enquiries — she was indeed pursuing her plan of opening a Home and hoped that everyone would join her willingly. The Governor already seemed content with the scheme and with co-operation and goodwill it should surely be possible for it to be in operation very soon.

She spent the next day arranging a new job and home for Flora, and once plans were well under way took leave of her friends and once again set off for the Parramatta ferry. This time she caught it without trouble, enjoyed a few days rest and returned to Sydney ready for a new round of fighting.[4]

Now her mind was made up. She would not attempt to run away from her work. She could not allow other girls to go the way of Flora and perhaps to be found only as the water receded at low tide.

One by one, though only slowly, the difficulties in her path began to be overcome. The biggest hurdle was that of sectarian bitterness — her Catholicism was still a major obstacle to many. Finally, however, it became possible to name a date on which the Home could be announced as open. Shortly before that day, Caroline took possession of the premises. Still short of funds, and of active supporters prepared to tackle the practical jobs that faced the project, she spent the first night there all alone.

Or, rather, not quite alone. As she was later to describe very graphically, just as she had settled down to sleep a large rat jumped on her shoulders, to be quickly followed by two more. She shook them off, and scrambled out of bed hurriedly. On a sudden inspiration she went to her small store of supplies, and prepared some slices of bread and butter, which, with a dish of water, she placed in the centre of the room, well away from her bed. Smelling the food, the rats headed for it at once. 'With a light by my side, I kept my seat on the bed, reading 'Abercrombie' and watching the rats until four in the morning' she remembered vividly later, 'I at one time counted thirteen, and never less than seven did I observe at the dish during the night.'[3] The next day, she obtained some rat poison in the form of arsenic, and put this on some more bread and butter, and then went through the performance again. 'Thus passed my first four nights in the home' she recalled grimly.

Once free of rats, the place was ready to receive its first immigrants. It was a wooden building, of which Caroline initially used only the storeroom until gradually the other rooms were made habitable. The barracks only ever provided the most rudimentary accommodation – but it was better than the street. And soon girls started to arrive to make use of it.

Caroline quickly found that a jobs register was not a difficult thing to run in Sydney – there was a good demand for girls willing to work with the settled families, and people started coming to the Home to make enquiries. Ladies who had helped her on the Committee were of course the first to use her services, and the word spread rapidly. But strength and determination were needed to cope with the immense practical problems from the very first day. Men of bad character started to hang around the Home, trying to chat to the girls and not infrequently returning to the back door once they had been sent away from the front. There was a major problem of night supervision. Caroline had by now engaged a Matron, who supervised all the domestic arrangements, but it was clear that further support was needed. For a while, she tried to maintain her own small establishment near the home with her three little boys, but it was no use. It was clear that she had to be personally present in the actual Home itself each night. With a heavy heart, she sent the children out to the suburbs, to be looked after by Miss Galvin. The plan was that after the initial problems of setting up the project had been solved and a system established she would be able to resume her own home life again. Until then, the sacrifice had to be made.

It was not done easily or lightly. At first only Archie, the oldest and the one most likely to get into trouble, went to Windsor to be with Miss Galvin. But after a short while it was clear that the others would have to follow. Caroline disliked the idea. What decided her was the ever present threat of fever and disease. She was working not only with girls in the Home but among the immigrants generally, many of whom were living in very squalid conditions. One night, a woman came to her with a pitiful request for a shroud 'to make her dead bairn decent'[4]. There were 94 girls sleeping in the barracks that night and the risks of infectious disease were great.

Yet the work prospered. Fairly soon the *Sydney Morning Herald* was reporting her success: 'It is only a few days since Mrs Chisholm obtained possession of the barracks, and since then she has procured situations for seven families at wages ranging from £21 to £26 a year, eleven children under thirteen years of age, from £2/10 to £7 a year, and seventy-six female servants at from £9 to £16 a year − of the latter fifty-eight were sent out into the country. A few persons have also obtained pecuniary assistance, and some donations of bread, coffee, tea, rice, sugar, etc. The religious instruction of the young women has not been lost sight of; those belonging to the Church of England are visited twice a week ...'[5]

The reference to work for children perhaps needs explaining. This was, of course, long before the days of compulsory universal education, and in most schools for the poorer classes the leaving-age was 12. So Caroline's obtaining jobs for children under 13 should be seen in this context. She was certainly not taking them away from their parents and sending them to become industrial slaves − most probably these children were orphans who would otherwise have roamed destitute. By placing them with families and guaranteeing them a wage as well as full board, she was providing for their future, and ensuring them of a protection and stability they would certainly never have found for themselves or expected from a workhouse in Britain. There were certainly a number of children who did need her help in this way — the illegitimate offspring of some of the convict women, and also children orphaned after arrival in the colony, for whom no provision had been made by the authorities.

However, the most important thing for the whole colony was not just to get jobs for people in Sydney, but to look to the immense possibilities that lay in the interior. There was employment to be had on the farms and homesteads — and these would be jobs with a long-term future. Families who had settled out in the wonderful countryside of New South Wales were creating whole new communities. There was abundant food, and prosperity resting on the thriving agriculture. The wives of the settlers needed help and companionship. The unmarried farmers needed wives. This was something that Caroline was beginning to realise, sometimes with humour and sometimes with real human pity. There was a gross disparity between the sexes throughout the colony — a legacy of the old transportation schemes and of current immigration policies. Little or no assistance had been given to respectable single women who might consider settling in Australia. It was more or less assumed that females were no use in the rough, raw colony. Men were needed to work the land and produce goods. But women and children were seen merely as a burden and an irritation.

All this had to change. Girls should be given help and encouragement to settle with families on the farms and home-steads. Once they had a stable home and job, they could make their own decisions about their future. Most would probably marry and have families. This must surely be the chief hope for the future stability of the colony. Already, Caroline had seen the aching loneliness written into the faces of so many of the men around Sydney. So many of them had faced terrible hardships but had eventually worked their way to respectability and had achieved a reasonably comfortable life — now they needed wives and children to give them a future and a hope.

News of the new job agency opened by Mrs Chisholm spread in the colony, and now people who came in from the outlying districts visited her. She started to gather information about the possibilities opening up. Soon it became plain that it would be worth sending out a group of girls with the next waggon train, and placing them with settled families. The local newspaper helped her enormously in this campaign, by urging its readers to bring in news about the jobs available, and to support the work of helping the young people to go off to the rural areas to take up the work available.

Gifts had begun to arrive at the Home, which were encouraging symbols of the community's support and enthusiasm for what Caroline was trying to do. Food – practical things like flour and tea – was donated. There were offers of help with transport and with contacts in the outlying areas. It was clear that in her desire to help people, Caroline had truly struck a chord. This warmed her heart and encouraged her as she looked to the future.

'During the present and next months many hundred drays will visit Sydney from different parts of the interior' commented the *Sydney Morning Herald* 'and if the proprietors of those which will return empty or only partially loaded will render assistance in getting single women and families into the colony, they will be conferring great favours upon numerous individuals, and be doing a public benefit at comparatively small cost or inconvenience to themselves. We particularly call the attention of settlers to this.' The hint was taken, and there were promises of help in taking 'Mrs Chisholm's girls' to the interior.

But the bush, for all its promises, also held terrors for those newly arrived from England. Whereas Sydney was a settled town, with the appearance of a fully organised and structured community, the interior was untamed country. Here there were weird and wonderful animals, wide plains that stretched for miles, unexplored territories beyond the horizon, surging rivers and jagged mountains. There were also bushrangers, ready to prey on the undefended traveller. There was no shelter along the rough highway. There was the danger of getting lost in unmapped territory, of dying of thirst or hunger after straying from the only known road. No wonder that when Caroline first suggested to a group of girls that they should travel with the next group of bullock-waggons to leave Sydney for the interior, many simply refused to go.

Caroline herself was in fact keen to travel in her adopted country, and discover what life outside Sydney was really like. Letters and introductions through contacts were of limited use. It was far better to do her work through good personal links, creating a network based on real trust. She also had a very maternal feeling about some of the girls in her care, especially the youngest ones. They needed support and encouragement as they went ahead to new challenges. If the colony was to prove itself as a place of hope and opportunity then there must be a sense of community solidarity. Despite the needs of the Home in Sydney, she decided she would go out into the bush and open up this new chapter herself, rather than leaving it all to others, or to chance.

The Home was in good hands by now, with a system organised to deal with newcomers, and a structure from which the matron and other helpers would not deviate. The way ahead lay elsewhere. So as soon as she could, Caroline arranged to leave Sydney with a group of settlers, and to stay with the group until every girl had been settled. She would collect as much information as she could about life in the bush, and bring the news back to Sydney. She would also seize the opportunity of finding out about the wider issues affecting new colonists: how prosperous the farms were, the prices of crops, the sort of help and encouragement the settlers sought from both the local administration and the government back home (everyone still called it 'home') in Britain. Already, the difficulties and disadvantages of the present emigration system from Britain were only too apparent. Half-formed in Caroline's mind was the idea of collating information in order to produce some sort of report which could be sent back to London urging changes. Families were being broken up through the 'Bounty' system which effectively meant that people with large numbers of children were penalised by having to pay extra for their passage — even though they were precisely the people that the colony so badly needed. Many had left children with relatives in England or Ireland, hoping to send for them later.

There was a desperate need for more young women in Australia — and for a system through which they could travel under adequate protection and be met on arrival by people who would look after them. And there were the convicts who sought long-lost wives and children left behind in Britain, and who wanted so badly to bring them out to Australia.

All of this depended on looking at the great possibilities of the outback. This was Australia's great resource, which the colonial authorities in Britain must be made to recognise. As the waggon train set off along the road leading out of Sydney Caroline felt full of optimism. Here was sunshine, enthusiasm, and new hope. What had been a place of desolation for many, a colony of convicts with a culture based on violence, cruelty, hardship and hunger, must surely, eventually, turn into something quite different. The girls' chatter and exclamations as they noticed new sights, the creaking of the waggons and the cheery bustle of humans and animals on the move, gave the morning a sense of quickening excitement.

'The scenes enacted on these journeys can be imagined' says a subsequent pamphlet about the bush treks, 'the evening camp-fires, the grateful people going to their new lives and new homes, under guardianship of a woman who was as full of strength and resource as of the tender qualities of her womanhood.'[6]

It was indeed on these journeys that something akin to a legend came to be born. Caroline discovered that she had the gift of water-divining. No one knows why, but it is a fact that some people are able to 'feel' where water can be found underground, while others cannot.

Caroline never spoke about this gift for water-divining. Yet its significance was not lost on the trekkers. It contributed to the aura that had begun to surround Mrs Chisholm. When she knew there was water in a certain place, and urged the men to dig for it, there would be a moment of eye contact, of silence and uncertainty. Then someone would silently nod and begin, and one by one others would follow suit. When the water came bubbling up, Caroline was usually already busy with the cooking or some other task. She'd look over and barely acknowledge the cheers and sudden chatter that had greeted the discovery of water. She simply turned busily to the next task — but then later, especially when a quiet moment came against the background of the group talking and laughing and eating around the fire, she'd glance over to the spring and feel again the sense of awe, the puzzlement, and the mystery. She could not explain how she came to know the water was there. Yet she simply sensed, in a powerful, physical way, its undoubted presence.

After a long day's journeying, the evening meal — it was always meat, tea, and 'damper' — tasted good around the camp-fire, and then the company bedded down for the night near the waggons. Caroline usually found a place alongside her girls. There would be talking and whispering at first, going over the events of the day, planning and speculating for the next stage of the journey. But the travelling had been hard, and no one took long to settle down to rest.

The night sounds of the bush were all around them as they fell asleep, and the Southern Cross glittered down among the other stars in the sky. Reared in the English countryside, Caroline had known nothing like the vastness of this new territory, but now she loved it. She could sense its spell on the young people. How fresh it all felt! There was something lonely about it, but also something magnificent. And the wideness of the space made the human being somehow infinitely more precious. The companionship and the comradeship — what the old settlers called the 'mateship' of the bush — was something special to Australia.

Next day it was good, in the heat of the afternoon, to draw up at last beside some settler's farmhouse, with the family hurrying to meet the drays, and water being quickly drawn for tea, and a great clatter of talk and bustle and excitement. Here one or more of the newcomers would be settled, and over a meal news would be given of other nearby farms, other job opportunities. There would be generous gifts of food for the journey. The farming families were keen to hear news from Sydney — and to pass on their own news. Caroline took it all in, and wrote much down — about prices and land, hopes and plans, ideas and speculations. It was all grist to the mill as she sought ideas for the future.

At every farm the mood of welcome was the same — newcomers were a pledge of the future, of the land opening up and more prosperity on the way. As meat sizzled on a barbeque and perhaps some music started, the atmosphere would be festive and the conversation cheerful. It had become well known that Mrs Chisholm's waggon teams brought girls into the neighbourhood — which meant a whole new round of social life, with entertainment and neighbourly get-togethers, and maybe some weddings on the horizon. The farmer's wife had usually been keenly awaiting the arrival of the Chisholm waggon train, and had drawn on stores to provide a good spread of food. Life could be raw and lonely out in the bush with few companions, and here was an opportunity to relish company. One the return journey, there would usually be waggons laden with food to be sold in the town, and letters and messages to be delivered. With every trekking group that set out along the bush roads, new chains of communication were being forged.

Back in Sydney, there was still plenty of work to do. Caroline was always a meticulous keeper of records. Every gift brought into the Home was carefully listed, and accounts were kept so that there should be no question of money seeming to be wasted. But the major part of her work was maintaining a guardianship over the girls who were arriving with each new ship, and protecting them at the Home until they were well settled. She was becoming known as a mother-figure in the colony. Brothel-madams, and the men who made use of their services, knew her by sight and there were sometimes things muttered as they passed her in the street. She represented a threat to their way of life. There were times when Caroline needed all her courage and sense of conviction. She met each new ship that arrived in the harbour, to tell the girls on board about the Home and to let them know about good job opportunities. Not infrequently she had to compete with brothel-madams who were also jostling for their attention.

There was also the nagging worry of ensuring that the Home would not be the centre of any kind of scandal — whether through financial mismanagement or through some silly escapade on the part of one of the girls. There were plenty of people who, friendly enough on the surface, would nevertheless seize on any opportunity of enjoying a laugh at the expense of this Catholic lady who was trying to do so much good and had perhaps taken on a bit more than she could handle.

On the practical level, every day brought new challenges. It was not just a question of finding jobs for the newly-arrived girls, or of providing accommodation for them. There was the wider question of emigration policy − the conditions on the ships, the scope for dishonesty and for ill-treatment of passengers. Caroline was beginning to learn about the hardship and misery endured by many girls on the long sea journey from England. Bullying was rife on board some ships, and there was often grave moral danger to young unprotected girls. Some arrived in Australia pregnant, others were simply used and abandoned. One way to stop the bullying would be to take legal action. This would be difficult and expensive, but punishing one bullying captain or crew member might make a huge difference for years to come by sending a strong message to all those in charge of ships concerning what would, and would not, be tolerated.

One particularly bad case of bullying that had come to light was that of young Margaret Bolton on board the *Carthaginian*. She had been known for her strong moral principles, and for her refusal to make herself available to any members of the crew in the way that many other girls were doing. For this, on one particular night, she was taken up on the deck in her nightdress, tied to a chair, and drenched with buckets of icy water. The ship's doctor, nominally in charge of all such young girls, played a prominent part in the bullying. Both he and the captain had also been involved in other violent incidents. Margaret Bolton had become ill as a result of the night spent on the open deck in soaking clothes. Caroline was instrumental in starting an investigation, and the result was a court case in which both the doctor and the captain received terms of imprisonment. The case had far-reaching consequences. It resulted in a dramatically changed attitude among shipping companies, and posed a direct challenge to the bounty migration system which was so evidently open to abuse.

It was this wider emigration issue which Caroline next addressed. She launched a detailed questionnaire which was taken as widely as possible around the colony, enquiring about farming methods, job opportunities, crop successes, homes, incomes, and the lifestyles of the settlers. Her aim was to show the authorities in Britain the enormous potential of Australia, and at the same time to highlight the tragic injustices resulting from transportation and stress the vital need for free and well-supervised emigration.

Her job registry was open every day, and by paying a subscription of two shillings and sixpence (12p), a prospective employer could interview a girl and engage her through Mrs Chisholm. The system worked well. Caroline also received a good many postal enquiries, all of which had to be answered. The careful records that were being kept were now beginning to speak for themselves. People recognised that the Home was a respectable place offering good opportunities for hard-working people. But Mrs Chisholm was also getting something of a reputation as a matchmaker! The girls, once settled, almost invariably married, and one of the nicest of her experiences was the arrival at the Home of a cheerful former resident, now a recent bride, perhaps bringing a posy of flowers, or a piece of the wedding cake, as a thank-you gift to her benefactress. Caroline's efficient accounting ensured that all such visits were recorded − by the time the Home was finally closed, she was to note that 51 pieces of wedding cake had been received!

## Notes

1. Caroline Chisholm *Female Immigration Considered in a Brief Account of the Sydney Immigrants' Home*. London, 1842, quoted in *Fifty One pieces of wedding cake* by Mary Hoban, Lowden, Kilmore, Australia, 1973.
2. Ibid.
3. Quoted in *Fifty One Pieces of Wedding Cake*.
4. This incident with Flora is described by Caroline in detail in *Female Immigration Considered*.
5. as 1.
6. *Sydney Morning Herald* 2nd Dec 1841.

# Chapter Seven

# Something Achieved

Over the next few years, Caroline settled thousands of emigrants. She wrote a cookery leaflet for young bush wives (seven different ways to use the basic ingredients of meat and flour!). She lobbied for farming land to be sold off in smaller plots so that the poorer emigrant might have the chance to buy; and she recommended to such settlers a system in which several men combined together to pool their resources for the first few years and work the land together until such time as each earned enough to go his own way. She became a prolific correspondent to the Sydney newspapers, as well as a writer of endless letters to all sorts of people who needed her help. She was seen by many as the manager of a most successful and respectable marriage bureau. She was also the dispenser of much practical and down-to-earth advice to many young wives who sought her out to discuss their difficulties. Her fame spread throughout the colony.

She was driven on by a strong sense of urgency. There was something so tragic about this great, sunlit, potentially abundant land being a source of sorrow and deprivation instead of hope and fulfilment. Her priority was to transform the colony from a bleak, rough, raw territory where men struggled against nature and against each other, into a real community. She was working with the full support of all who had the best interests of that community at heart, but there were entrenched attitudes that needed to be changed, and many problems and challenges every step of the way.

The gravest problem of all was the prejudice against families. A commentator on the Australian scene, writing about it for a readership back in London, noted: 'Settlers and squatters will never engage, if they can help it, men with families of children;

75

the support of the useless mouths they do not like; so it is advisable that immigrants should have as few encumbrances as possible. The morality of the bush might and would be much improved, if woman was more frequently there, but that is out of the question, if, on first arrival, they are surrounded by a number of young children; a master will avoid them, as he would a black snake, for he "does not wish to support, and bring up other people's children'".[1]

Another commentator made the same point: 'In some instances "wives" are patronized but "children" never. Advertisers want "men" and sometimes their "wives" without "incumbrance". Children are an incumbrance in a country where a bounty, a serious bounty, has to be paid on their importation. Penuriousness, or poverty, must dictate such advertisements, not patriotism.'[2]

Caroline was aware that great evils resulted from this refusal to acknowledge the reality and importance of family life.

Clergymen referred obliquely to the moral depravity of the colony, but were powerless to do anything about it while its greatest cause remained unremedied. They referred to some of the crimes by name: drunkenness, fighting, dishonesty, lack of neighbourly concern. But there were other sins not mentioned by name, but known to exist. 'Among the convicts, especially those incarcerated at Norfolk Island and other penal stations, sodomy had been very common, as it must be wherever large numbers of men are segregated for long periods. Most contemporary writers were silent upon the subject of sodomy in the outback, but none denied its prevalence and a few hinted broadly that it was common among the old hands and tended to spread to other elements of the tribe.'[3]

The solution to this was not only to settle more women and families out in the interior, but also to spread the message about what was being done, and about the happy results. It was also necessary to challenge the official thinking at a high level. Caroline began to develop ideas for sending back to London a detailed assessment of the whole emigration scene, based on a questionnaire distributed throughout the colony.

First, she wanted to tell the good news about her work with the girls whom she was placing in jobs. The Sydney Home and agency were now well known. Why not publish a small book about them? It might sell well, and be an advertisement for her work. So Caroline produced *Female Immigration considered, in a Brief Account of the Sydney Immigrants' Home*, which was published by James Tegg and printed in Sydney in 1842. It relied chiefly on its personal stories for its success. Caroline recounted the early struggles to start the home, and also described the cases of many of the different girls who had come to her. Few readers can resist a good human story. The book sold in good numbers, and she had created a little bit of history. It was the first book by a woman to be published in Australia.

Collecting together information to send back to the Colonial Office in London was a project which would take much more time, and required much patience and effort. Caroline drew up a very detailed list of questions, and started to gather information whenever she travelled about on her bush journeys.

These journeys were now aided and encouraged by many throughout the colony. She had been given a beautiful white horse, whom she named Captain, and this enabled her to ride ahead of the main party to visit homesteads, gather information, or prepare for the reception of a large group of people. Donations of food and other equipment continued to make the journeys financially secure. People seemed to want to outdo one another in generosity. Bills were paid, gifts presented, and a great deal of encouragement given. When a team of 'Mrs Chisholm's people' departed from Sydney, it did so amid cheers and goodwill. When it arrived at some distant outstation, there was a great excitement. Meat would be barbecued for the hungry new arrivals, and accommodation made ready for them where they could sleep that night. Caroline had now acquired a covered waggon and she always slept in or under this with a group of the youngest girls. During the long rides each day, she sometimes took a small child with her on Captain, to give its mother a break. On one occasion when a swollen river held up the party, the horse took children slowly across, ferrying them carefully two at a time, while the adults managed the waggons.

When she collected information from settlers, Caroline took it down verbatim. Some wrote it themselves, but many could not read or write. She copied faithfully exactly what they said, preserving all their colloquial expressions, jokes and mannerisms. Some of the stories were very heart-rending, especially when convict men spoke about the wives they had left behind in England or Ireland and desperately wanted to see again.

Caroline was giving a voice to a people. The Australian nation was in the process of being born, out here in the lonely bush. As the years went by, the stories of the early settlers would become part of folklore. She was the first to set it all on record: the early hardships, the success of farming, the hardships of the convict days and the sense of optimism that abounded as soon as settlers were allowed a fair chance to get on with their lives.

The chief facts which emerged were the sorrow of divided families, and the pressing desire of many people to be reunited with their relatives. Many also wanted to send money back to England or Ireland to help their families who might not come to Australia, but who should not be left in poverty. What was also very clear was the cruelty and savagery of the whole transportation system, and the abundant evidence of the value of a sound balanced alternative based on family emigration. What Australia needed were settlers who arrived with hope and courage, not shiploads of beaten men.

There had been for many years a system of official provision for sending out wives to join convict husbands, but it had always been difficult to administer, given the problems of communication over such large distances. Now, with transportation officially coming to an end, the Government back in Britain seemed to be washing its hands of the problem entirely. It would take determination and effort to ensure justice for the remaining convicts and their wives. There must also be a great campaign to assist young women coming out to Australia. Many of the single men spoke very tenderly of how much they would love to be married and raise a family. They would often show Caroline their comfortable cabins, and their stocks of food, and speak of how they would love to share it with a wife. Caroline recorded their statements. There was a chivalry about much of what they said that was very appealing. It was not possible to dismiss these men as merely rough settlers who had nothing to offer, or who should be treated as being somehow on a level with beasts.

Above all, Caroline loved to meet girls whom she had helped earlier on, and who were now happily married themselves. It was heart-warming to be welcomed into a simple cabin home, and given tea and damper, and shown the new baby, and asked about news. The more families settled in an area, the better the girls liked it. Loneliness, even for married people, was a big problem in the bush. The lonely 'squatters stations' must be made a thing of the past. A community life was needed, and this grew of its own accord once settlers established themselves. Homes eventually produced schools, churches, and social gatherings of every kind. Children grew up and married. Rough tracks became established routes, and roads were built linking farms and townships.

Everything that she saw on these bush journeys encouraged Caroline in her staunch belief that Australia's future lay in a rural-based economy. She warned people about the dangers of trying to stay on in Sydney and get casual work instead of having the courage to move out. Many young lives that started in optimism ended in despair in Sydney. There simply was not the work to be had, or the opportunities for acquiring a home. The lure of the bars was superficially attractive, but it did not offer long-term security.

It was important that the Colonial Office in London knew about her work in order that official support might not be lacking when it was needed. Sir George Gipps allowed Caroline to send a copy of her questionnaire in a despatch to London, and in due course a reply came from Lord Stanley at the Colonial Office in distant Downing Street. It was dated 31st May 1844 and read:

'I have read your despatch dated 12 December last, no 207 enclosing a letter addressed by Mrs Chisholm to the Colonial Land and Emigration Commissioners, accompanied by the forms of certain queries, designed to collect information in the Colony of New South Wales, on the subject of Immigration, together with answers which have already been obtained to some of these queries. I have communicated on this subject with the Emigration Commissioners.

'You will acquaint Mrs Chisholm that, although the questions contained in her letter appear to me well selected, and answers to many of them interesting, yet that, in order to render them useful for general purposes, a very extensive collection would be necessary; and it would also be requisite to digest the result into something of a Tabular form; and considering moreover that some of the information, such as Rates of wages and current prices in the Colony is already obtained and forwarded to this Country periodically, I have not felt myself at liberty to sanction any further expenditure than that which the local Government have already thought it necessary to incur on this subject.

'You will, at the same time, express to Mrs Chisholm the high sense, which I entertain of the valuable and benevolent services which she has rendered to the Emigrants of New South Wales.'

This was not wholly a disappointment to Caroline. It was inevitable that the Government in London should fail to sense the urgency and the importance carried in the earnest human statements that she had collated with such care. She still planned to publish her 'Voluntary Statements from the People of New South Wales' in Sydney, and meanwhile it was something to know that at least her name and the knowledge of her work had been communicated to the seat of power. It gave her a contact on which she could build.

She had more important matters on her mind. By the time Governor Sir George Gipps had handed her this despatch she was no longer working alone. Archibald had returned to her. He sailed back to Sydney from India in March 1845, after retiring from the Army early on health grounds. The reunion at Sydney must have been a touching one. He had left behind a young wife and small sons in a new land. Now he was being welcomed back by a confident family, well settled in the colony, and playing a most active part in its public life.

Caroline had much to tell him. Together they could now turn their attention joyfully to quiet family matters, enjoying each others' company and working out their long-term future plans.

One obvious idea was a return to England. Not only were there pressing family reasons for this — they had not seen their relatives for a great many years — but Caroline had certain specific duties to fulfil. She had been entrusted with so much vital information which must be drawn to the attention of the colonial authorities in London. Fascinated by her achievements, Archibald was to prove a most stalwart and loyal supporter in her work from this moment onwards. He assisted her in collating the huge amount of material she had prepared, and together they made plans about the tasks that needed to be tackled in England.

There were the many ex-convicts who desperately wanted her to locate their wives, children, or other relatives and bring them back to Australia. There were families who had been split up under the 'Bounty' system and who wanted to be reunited. This would mean tracking down children who had been left behind with various relatives and arranging for them to be sent to Australia by a specially chartered ship. There was the urgent necessity of burying for ever the last remnants of the old transportation system. The Colonial Office must be shown the practical advantages of a fair and just emigration system — one which put families as a priority, and ensured that ordinary hard-working people were given help and encouragement in making a fresh start for themselves in a new land.

Not long after Archibald's return, the 'Voluntary Statements' were published in Sydney and brought renewed encouragement to Caroline from many quarters that she should carry the message back to the Government in London. She was certainly determined to do so.

Caroline and Archibald took time and thought in planning the long journey. Before they left, Caroline was honoured publicly in Sydney, with a special gathering held to offer the thanks of the community, and warmest praise poured out in the press. She knew that she was carrying the hopes of many as she made the journey home. She was seen as Australia's unofficial ambassadress.

The only jarring note in all her years of achievement had been the occasional anxiety felt by some sections of the community concerning her religious beliefs. A fellow crusader in the cause of fair and just emigration was the

Revd Dr J.D. Lang. He had co-operated with Caroline on many projects, and given support to her Immigrants Home. But he remained convinced to the last that she was an unwitting agent of sinister Roman Catholicism, a dupe of the clergy and a person being used for dark schemes through which this new colony would be handed over to Papal control. Her concern for Irish girls was seen as particularly worrying. 'The irony was' as a commentator would later point out 'that Mrs Chisholm was born an English Protestant, but converted to Roman Catholicism when she married a Scottish Highlander of that persuasion'.[4]

In vain Caroline protested that she was not lobbying for one particular religious group, but genuinely seeking the good of all. Letters on the subject in the press continued to reverberate right up to the time that she left Australia for London. Some people were convinced for years that there was a definite 'Catholic plot' concerning the future of Australia, and that she was part of it.

In fact, Caroline was a deeply patriotic woman whose loyalty to Britain and to fostering good links between Australia and the 'old country' were strong. Her concern for immigrants was based on humanitarian concerns, motivated by a religious faith that was deeply sincere, but did not seek to use every opportunity for conversion in the way imagined. She was certainly not sympathetic to the cause of Irish nationalism, but as an Army officer's wife she was proud to affirm her loyalty to a United Kingdom of which she automatically saw Ireland as a part.

The religious controversy would never go away: it was deeply rooted in the position given to Dr Lang and to Caroline Chisholm by history. It would be several generations before the fears and prejudices on all sides of Britain and Australia's religious divisions altered. Meanwhile, all that Caroline could do was protest her innocence of any sinister intent, and to beg for sufficient tolerance so that she could pray in the way she had chosen. She was never, throughout her public life, ever to ally herself with any specifically Catholic group even when put under pressure to do so. From start to finish she would remain faithful to her early commitment to help all, regardless of creed.

Many years later an Australian author was to sum up her achievements: 'Mrs Chisholm was a woman who saw clearly what needed doing, and then did it, for she was deterred by no difficulties. Her thorough kindness of heart and complete self-abegnation eventually won their way with everyone who came into contact with her, but she could never have done a tithe of the great work she did if she had not had great powers of organisation, and that divine commonsense which is the best kind of wisdom. She was fortunate in her husband, who encouraged her and worked with her in every possible way. No greater woman has been connected with Australia.'[5]

## Notes

1. J. C. Byrne, *Twelve Years Wanderings*, London 1984
2. Richard Howitt *Impressions of Australia Felix during Four Years' Residence in that Colony*. London, 1845.
3. Russel Ward, *The Australian Legend*, Melbourne, 1958.
4. Malcolm D. Prentis, *The Scots in Australia*, Sydney, 1983.
5. Percival Serle, *Dictionary of Australian Biography*, Angus and Robertson, Sydney, 1949.

# Chapter Eight

# London

When Caroline and Archibald left Sydney to return to England they carried with them not only much goodwill and many hopes, but also a sum of money raised by public subscription – one hundred and fifty guineas – which had been presented as a thank-you gift by the people of New South Wales. This money, and Archibald's modest pension, would be all that they had to live on over the next few years. They in fact spent much of their own money on Caroline's work, for she never received any salary, and most of the people she helped were so poor that there was no question of receiving payment from them.

The journey was to prove a difficult one. Caroline was now expecting their fourth child. Their joy at this news was tempered by the worry about how to cope: they had very much wanted to avoid a birth at sea and tried to plan a sailing that would get them to England before the baby was due. However, delays meant that eventually they had to sail on the *Dublin* in the spring of 1846, and the length of the journey meant that the baby would be born during the journey.

Although Caroline was confident and in good health, she still approached the birth with some dread. It proved a difficult and frightening experience. Every help was offered: kind women passengers took care of the other children, the cabin was made as comfortable as possible, and privacy ensured. Nothing, however, could be done about the constant motion of the ship, the cramped conditions, the smells, and the lack of important medical equipment. The birth was a difficult one, and left Caroline exhausted and ill – although glad to be the mother of another baby son.

Frail and weak, she was unable to feed the child, who survived because of milk provided by the ship's goat. Other passengers willingly gave up their own milk rations to ensure that there was enough. The child was baptised with the name Sydney, in honour of Australia. Everyone on board took an interest in him, and shared in a sense of pride and pleasure as both he and his mother steadily improved.

On the last few days of the journey, Caroline was well enough to leave her cabin and walk about a little. Archibald took charge of all the preparations for disembarkation, supervising trunks and tickets, money, children, lists and hand luggage. He was attentive, and was at her side whenever she wanted any sort of support. The baby was much admired, and the other children praised for their good behaviour and helpfulness during the voyage.

Exhausted, unwell, but glad to be alive, Caroline left the ship on Archibald's arm to find the best possible news awaiting them. Her mother, to whom she had of course written announcing their arrival, had hastened to London to greet the ship and would take charge of all domestic cares while she recuperated. The reunion between mother and daughter was an emotional one. The Caroline whom Mrs Jones had last seen had been a young bride, excited by the adventure of a prospective trip to India. Now she was the mother of four children, and an experienced traveller who had seen the Australian bush, given birth at sea, and was about to embark on a whole new life in London. As they embraced, Caroline felt wrapped in a sense of new security and strength.

Mrs Jones, for her part, had been a busy grandmother, watching the offspring of Caroline's various brothers and sisters grow up. Now most of them were safely embarked on lives of their own. Caroline, as her youngest child, naturally had a special place in her heart – and she was excited about seeing Caroline's children, known to her only through letters. She was only too happy to take on the task of helping the family settle into a new life in England.

With four small children – Archie, William, Henry and baby Sydney – and only modest funds, the Chisholms looked for a suitable family home that would suit their needs and not be a drain on resources. They settled not far from the docks –

at 29 Prince Street, in Mile End. This was very far from being a smart address. It lay in the East End, on the edge of a teeming community that fringed the City of London — Whitechapel, Stepney, Bow, and the whole of the area in the great loop of the river around the docks.

This was a world which the writer Charles Dickens — whom Caroline was to get to know well — was to immortalise in his novels. It was a world of poverty and struggle, of fascinating characters, humour, strong traditions, crime, special loyalties, and a unique way of speaking. By settling here, Caroline would be right among the people she most needed to meet — the ordinary London poor from whom so many of the Australian settlers had come.

This was a London which was the confident capital of a thriving trading nation which was building an empire for itself around the world. It could not be more different from Sydney. It boasted factories and rows of streets densely-packed with housing, shops and offices, banks and Government buildings, medieval and Wren churches, famous monuments and centres of art, music, and education. Here Parliament sat and Queen Victoria lived — the same Parliament and Queen whose writ ran in far Australia. Here decisions would be made which could affect the lives of all those far-away colonists.

The Chisholms' house in Mile End, was off Commercial Road, which led into the City, the banking and commercial centre of the English-speaking world. It was near the great London docks, where ships brought goods from all over the globe. This was a poor but bustling area of London — a far cry from the smarter areas of Belgravia or Mayfair. The Thames rolled along nearby, its grey waters often evil-smelling in summer because of the sewage pumped into them from all over London. The river curled its way past the City, and along to Westminster, where Parliament sat and the Government offices were.

Caroline knew that she must introduce herself formally to Earl Grey, the Colonial Secretary. He already knew of her, but now they must establish a sound working relationship. There were so many different topics that she wanted to tackle that it was hard to know where to start. She began with an introductory letter, by way of establishing herself and setting the scene for the work ahead.

'My Lord' she began, writing in a firm clear hand with occasional flourishes for capital letters. The establishment of communication with Lord Grey was to be as important as the original meeting with Governor Sir George Gipps back in New South Wales some years previously. It was important to make the correct impression. The letter was a long one, and set out the whole picture of Australian settlement and its problems:

'It may not be unknown to your Lordship that I interested myself for a period of eight years in New South Wales in trying to ameliorate the condition of Emigrants on their arrival there, and other classes of the community who wanted employment, and that your late predecessor in office was pleased to tender to me his thanks in his despatch of the 3rd May 1844, to the Govt of New South Wales, for the services which I had rendered to Emigrants. The knowledge which I have thus gained, of the capabilities of the Colony, and of the character of the inhabitants, from my having travelled in the remote interior, in my exertions to settle individuals and locate families, emboldens me to address you at present on the important subject of Emigration, and on the evils that press so heavily upon the social and moral advancement of that Colony.

'During the present lamentable distress that afflicts parts of the United Kingdom, particularly Ireland [she was referring to the appalling Irish famine, of which more later], I cannot in duty refrain from bringing to Your Lordship's notice for the information of Her Majesty's Government the numerous and daily Applications which I receive, from Country Labourers and whole families, for a free Passage to New South Wales and Port Phillip, and more particularly from the relatives of those who had migrated to Australia some years ago and who have written to me at the request of their friends, the majority of these are from Ireland. On Monday last the Applications for that day amounted to three hundred, and when I retrospectively look to the vast and suitable field which New Holland offers for the enterprising and industrious emigrant, I cannot but grievously lament, if the earnest solicitations of those poor people are not conceded to, viz, a free Passage to New South Wales.

'One of the evils which I would take the liberty to press upon your Lordship's notice, and that of Her Majesty's Government, is the frightful disparity of the sexes (men being out of all proportion in number to women) and from which flows misery and crime, I need not dwell upon, and to this unnatural anomaly of the human race in that colony, may be traced in great degree that gradual but certain extermination of those unfortunate tribes, the Aborigines of New Holland; the original holders of this soil, demand the speedy and parental interference of a humane Government.

'With a hope of removing to some extent this crying and National evil, I beg most respectfully to say that I would feel disposed to co-operate in finding a remedy, by making a selection of young women of good character as free emigrants to Australia.

'I beg most deferentially to remark that the present policy of sending women under penal sentence to New South Wales only adds infinitely to the moral evil, and it is with gratification I have to observe that I never met but with one man who did not express extreme desire to be married to a woman of good character, and it is a most erroneous opinion that such women make suitable wives enough for reclaimed convict men; nature and moral religion both shrink from the idea of such characters as the mothers of children – no one is more sensitive on that point than a reformed prisoner received back into the social order of society, and often in my travels through the Bush did I come upon the solitary and cheerless Hut of the unfortunate Emancipist living alone, or at times two young men associated together, because they could not meet with respectable females to whom they could offer otherwise a comfortable home. And I also frequently fell in with Natives of Australia, descendants of Europeans, similarly situated – no helpmate to cheer their habitations. It may also be observed that respectable Emigrant parents object to their daughters serving in the same establishment with this class of females.

'The demand for domestic servants by respectable families in Australia, and by the yeomen of the country, renders it easy to provide for such young women, as may be disposed to emigrate, soon after their arrival, more particularly as the demand for servants in the interior is on the increase. The protection necessarily to be afforded to those young females on their passage out, as well as on their arrival in the Colony, and after dispersion in the interior, is a subject of such paramount importance to their welfare, that it will afford me deep and sincere satisfaction to impart that information in knowledge which I have gained relative thereto from experience.'

This was an impassioned letter. Although she signed herself formally 'your very obdet. and Humbe Servt.' in the accepted abbreviated but obsequious style, she was writing from the heart. Her point about the Aborigines was one on which she felt very strongly, and will be developed later. The wealth of colourful detail with which she surrounded her comments on the plight of lonely ex-convicts was to be typical of many letters. She knew that she was writing of a distant colony that seemed utterly remote to an English politician whose lifestyle focused around a large comfortable London house, Parliamentary sessions, perhaps a club, pleasant dinners with political talk in elegant dining rooms, and gatherings in beautiful country houses. To bring home the reality of Australia, she must draw on her experiences there − experiences virtually unique and certainly unknown to someone like Lord Grey. She must make him understand the grim misery of the 'solitary and cheerless hut', the crudity of convict women corrupting young girls, the savagery with which the Aborigines had been treated and the anxiety and sorrow of people forced to migrate through economic circumstances but determind to carry their respectability and their moral values with them.[1]

The letter was duly stamped at the Colonial Office 'received Jan 27 1847' and there was a note that it should be referred to the 'L and E Commissioners'. This meant the Colonial Land and Emigration Commissioners, the official body in charge of emigration matters. In due course a great many of Mrs Chisholm's letters were to land on their desks, and over the years she was to be regarded as being almost as much of an authority on emigration as they were. But meanwhile, with this first letter, Lord Grey asked that they be instructed to 'devise any practicable measure for effecting the object in view' while 'Mrs C. must be thanked for the communication, express my sense of the benevolence of her object and my desire to promote its accomplishment, at the same time inform her that her letter has been referred to the Cmm and request her to communite with them.'

Caroline was writing at a critical time and her letter was effective. Matters in Ireland became more tragic by the day. Later that same Spring, a parish priest from Ballyleague, near Lanesborough, described graphically, in a letter to *The Tablet*, the horrors of the famine. The high rents and absentee landlords, the injustices under which the people lived, and the failure of the potato crop which had formerly provided them with a basic food, had brought death and misery:

'I witness four or five deaths daily within this parish from mere famine' wrote Father Patrick McPadden 'and others who labour for a small remuneration on the public works in a few days become exhausted and fall victims also, as the trifle they receive for their labour goes to support the weak of their family, while they themselves sink under the weight and become as bad as those who have no employment'. He described finding rat-eaten corpse in one house, and people eating weeds and grass out of sheer starvation, even though they knew them to be poisonous. 'Out of a vast, religious, humble and truly charitable congregation, I could not number fifty around our chapel altar on Easter Sunday, all being dead or weakened by hunger, or having parted with their wretched clothes, could not attend' he wrote. 'Our fields are untilled, and the hum of the cheerful cottager, and the prattle of his innocent children, are heard no more. One far and wide-spread mass of misery and desolation extends through the land; and in place of peace and plenty, nothing reigns but a low, still, putrid scene of famine and plague.'[2]

Another priest, Father James Browne from Ballintubber, Ballyglass, County Mayo, described a similar picture: 'Some have perished from hunger in the ditches; some have dropped dead in the open fields; some have been found dead on the wayside; some in barns and outhouses. One boy was found dead in a forge; whole families have been swept away.'

Caroline knew all about this from first-hand accounts by people who had fled from the hunger to England and were now seeking her out to beg for information about emigration to Australia. Already her name was known. People in Australia had been sending messages to relatives urging them to contact Mrs Chisholm, because she would find a way to help them reach the land of plenty that awaited them over the ocean. Caroline was also kept informed through her Church. Catholics throughout the rest of Britain had received a special message begging for help, in the form of a Pastoral Letter which was read out at all Masses. They had responded generously. Collections were made in all the churches. In London the historic church in Warwick Street collected £245, the poor mission of St George's across the river in Southwark over £200, and several others over £100 each. These were substantial sums from a small Catholic community mostly made up of people who were by no means well-off.[3]

But if Caroline wanted to be of immediate practical help in the field of emigration, she must tackle specific projects rather than generalities. Once her contact with Lord Grey had been established, she started to deal with the various specific projects she had in mind. There were three immediate priorities. She must obtain free transport for convicts' wives who wanted to join their husbands in Australia. She must contact the various 'bounty children' – spread all over Britain and Ireland – who had been left behind when their families sailed and whose parents now desperately sought them. And she must do all she could to establish a proper emigration pattern, helping to improve the male/female disparity by sending over young girls in the care of someone who would ensure that they received proper protection during the voyage.

From the first day that the Chisholms arrived, the house in Mile End had been turned into an office as well as a home. Here Caroline worked on her correspondence, and, with the domestic arrangements made for the day, settled down to her work. She had at this stage no secretarial help of any kind, and no financial assistance. Her work would inevitably involve much travelling because she needed to track down the missing relatives of (often illiterate) families who wished to be reunited in Australia.

Fortunately, travel was easier now than it had been in the England she had left in the 1830s. The railways had arrived — despite all the opposition from many landowners and farmers, the tracks now carried passengers with amazing speed from one major city to another, transforming the lives of many in the process.

Caroline was modern-minded enough to use every possible new convenience, and efficient enough to ensure that her office work was as streamlined as possible. Letters were carefully anotated and kept, facts noted, information checked. She knew only too well that many people hundreds of miles away were placing an enormous amount of hope and trust in her efforts. They were mostly people who were poor, had suffered much, and were caught up in injustices which were not of their own making. She must not let them down.

'My Lord' she wrote from Prince's Street, Jubilee Place, Mile End, on 21st January 1847 to Lord Grey: 'In doing myself the honour of transmitting for your Lordship's human consideration the Petition of eighteen Heads of Families, amounting in all to seventy souls, being the Wives and Children of men who have been transported some years ago to New South Wales but who have since, through reformation of character, regained their freedom, or hold 'tickets of leave', I beg most respectfully to express a hope that you will be pleased to grant a Free Passage to New South Wales to those unhappy Wives and Children who have thus been separated from their natural protectors for so many years.'

She did not hesitate to use her status as a woman, wife and mother, to affirm the importance — even the sanctity — of family bonds. Her appeal was on the grounds of humanity, morals, and common sense. She wrote in a firm, clear hand, and had a very distinctive signature, with two large curls swirling beneath the 'C' of Caroline, and another one under the 'C' of Chisholm. 'In submitting their Application', she went on, 'I take the liberty to remark that my residence in New South Wales for eight years enables me to state, that as a body the Emancipatists of that Colony are entitled, from their uniform good and peaceable contact, to very kind consideration on the part of Her Majesty's Government, and that those poor men, who had left Families behind them, never lost the hope, but that the Boon which they now seek, would one day be granted to them, through the indulgence of a human Government.'[4]

But at this stage she was still learning her way around Government departments. This letter was annotated 'Petition retained in Dept. Returned to Mrs Chisholm. NB The List should have been sent to the HO at first.' So off it presumably went to the Home Office, and thus began the crusade to link up the convicts with their families. Caroline had to do a great deal of research work to track down the various people involved. In a world without carbon paper, telephones, fax machines, or photocopiers – documentation took time, patience and effort. Letters had to be copied out two or three times by hand, and records kept in ledgers with cross-reference filing systems. It took a great deal of laborious effort to ensure that the necessary information went back and forth as things were checked.

'With reference to your letter enquiring for William Holmes', Caroline was writing to Benjamin Hawes at the Colonial Office on February 6th 'I have the honor [she used the old spelling, today regarded as American in style] to state that I know four men of that name who were sent out by Her Majesty's Govt: one is an Englishman and he lives in the Port Maiquarie and New England district and is a 'ticket of leave' and I am inclined to think is the William Holmes enquired after, as he is a small settler, but works occasionally as the neighbouring settlers' dwelling, as a Bricklayer.

'I met William Holmes in the Gungadai District, about 350 miles in the Interior of the Colony, who was most anxious to hear from his friends, and at his entreaty, I enquired at the Post Office Sydney, and found a letter for him which I forwarded by private hand – the difficulty of communicating by post is very great for persons employed in the remote Districts – the impression on my mind is, that this man was an Englishman.

'As the most certain mode of satisfying the parental anxiety of Mrs Holmes whose letter you have had the humanity to forward to me, I have taken the liberty of enclosing a letter which, if forwarded by Mrs Holmes, will meet with every attention.'[5]

For many years, the position had been that a convict's family could communicate with him, once he had been transported to Australia, only with the greatest difficulty. Often they did not know where he was in that vast remote colony. A special grey form was available, which could be folded and posted as a letter: its printed instructions indicated that if the convict's address in Australia was not known, it was sufficient to put the name of the ship in which he had been transported. A warning was added that on no account was any enquiry to be made until at least a year had elapsed from the posting of the letter. This was because of the time that had to be allowed for the letter to get to Australia by the slow sea journey, be finally delivered to the right person, and a reply posted back.

Caroline was driven by the knowledge of the hardship and loneliness that had been endured for so long by so many people. Finally the Home Office granted 'A free passage to the families of certain emancipated and ticket-of-leave men ... in the Female Convict Ship *Asia* ... to take them to Hobart Town on their way to New South Wales'. This was one thing accomplished. But by the time Caroline heard that news, she was already busy with her next project − the sending out of the 'Bounty Children'. In fact, it was planned that some of the travellers might even overlap.

Collecting together information on the 'bounty children' proved extremely difficult and time-consuming. Having extracted a Government commitment to funding their voyage out to Australia, Caroline encountered repeated difficulties. By comparison, obtaining permission for the convicts' wives and families to travel out had been easy.

Almost all the children involved were in Ireland. This increased the administrative problems involved in tracking them down and ensuring that letters addressed to their guardians or last known addresses actually reached them.

The Colonial Land and Emigration Commissioners opened a file[6] on all the children, who would sail in the *Sir Edward Parry* to New South Wales. Slowly, the information was collected together, and the administrative details sorted out. Sometimes finding a child was a straightforward matter of writing to the known guardian and obtaining a firm commitment that he or she would be ready to travel. These were the cases that proved easiest to organise. Thus Thomas Poole wrote from Mayfield on May 31st in response to a query about 'J. Joyce's children': 'Joyce had been my steward for 20 years, all his children were born within my demesne, and I have known them all from their infancy. Emmanuel went to America two years since, and is there still. Henry and Anne have been living within a few miles of my house: they are both in good health and anxious and ready to join their Parents. You will please to let me know what Outfit they will require and when they should go to Plymouth they are both very well conducted respectable persons.'

But other cases were far more problematic. One page in the Commissioners' file was devoted to details of children who for one reason or another declined to go. In a neat list, with the child's name, parents' names, and other information, was written the reason for the child not going. It made sad reading. The reasons included: 'Child would prefer not to go' 'Is in America' 'Is dead' (very common) 'Will not leave his guardian' (also very common) 'Guardian refuses to send her' (again very common) 'are apprenticed (against the names of two children from one family) 'child refuses to leave Ireland' and 'is too young for voyage at present'. Individual letters also told the stories: 'Sir', wrote Henry Prettie from Tullamedan Rectory on May 8th (1847), 'In reply to yours of the 3rd Inst, I beg to state, that having made the necessary inquiry relative to Michael Butler, the Child named in your letter he has been dead for the last three years. The Grandfather, with whom he was left, did not mention the event in any of his letters.'

Sometimes people in charge of the children seemed to be acting very cruelly. One letter, from a Board of Guardians of a Workhouse, stated that the boy concerned was apprenticed to a watchmender and was thus bound to that firm until the age of 21. But there were other cases where the objection was an understandable one. John Conray wrote from Ballinasloe on 27th June: 'In reference to your letter directed from the Emigration Office, Westminster, concerning the Child named in the Margin, John Conroy, I would of course send him to his Father if he would consent to go; but to be candid with you he would not go on any account. Now how could I send such a Child without either guide or guardian or anyone to protect him. The next opportunity we will send him.' This writer was reassured that proper protection would be given during the entire voyage. There were more dramatic scenes. John Crowe, a farmer from Knockaderren wrote 'I can state to you that Kitty Minehan is the daughter of Pat Minehan who emigrated to New South Wales in 1841. She is only about eight years next Christmas Day. She is in good health at present, and the time since her Parents left her in care of Bridget Kief, parish of Killoloe, county of Clare. On the first day of July I went to Bridget Kief's house, and I ask Kitty Minehan would she go to her Parents. Answer no. I caught her by the hand, and said she should. She began to cry, nor neither can she clothe herself nor pay her passage to Plymouth. Bridget Kief only said she would not let her go until she should get some money for her support. They are very poor living on one pound of meal each of them in the day.'[7]

In the end, only about half of the children whom Caroline had been asked to find eventually went to Australia. Money had to be obtained out of public funds to provide clothes for many of them: in a number of cases there were not only insufficient clothes for the long journey to Australia but even for a journey to England to join the ship at Plymouth. Arrangements were made to meet a group of the children in Dublin and obtain outfits for them there before taking them on. Meanwhile the *Sir Edward Parry* was being prepared. A Dr Sullivan was appointed Surgeon to supervise the children's health on board and a Mrs Read Head Matron. The ship sailed from Plymouth in September. Its passengers would disembark at Port Phillip and at Sydney, and the families would have to travel from the various parts of New South Wales to meet them at one or other of these ports.

Caroline was deeply involved with every detail of this whole venture. At first, it had seemed virtually impossible that it would ever be brought to fruition. Back in February the Land and Emigration Commissioners saw enormous problems and difficulties, pointing out that 'the chances of Infantile disease, which may turn in crowded ships to Epidemic fever, and the trying nature of the kinds of food on which to a certain extent they must depend at sea, greatly multiply the risks of misfortune.' In the end Earl Grey's official authority in favour of a modified scheme for sending out the children had to be sought. The Commissioners did not want to take the decision themselves: 'We are embarrassed by the hopes which have been raised amongst the Parents in the Colony, and their relatives in this Country, and are anxious to be guided by higher authority in the decision whether it is a greater evil on the one hand to disappoint these hopes; or on the other hand to attempt to fulfil them under a certain amount of ... difficulty.'[8]

Even when Lord Grey had given the scheme the go-ahead, the huge practical problems remained. 'The children, with 3 or 4 exceptions are scattered over Ireland where no shipping is to be had for New South Wales' wrote Mr S. Walcott of the Colonial Land and Emigration Commissioners on May 21st. He then outlined the plan that was eventually set in motion: 'to endeavour to collect at Plymouth as many of the children as can pay for their necessary outfit and to contract by Public Tender for there passage from that Port, providing a Matron to take charge of the Females, a Schoolmaster with other requisite attendants, and a Surgeon to superintend the whole party ...'

But once it was all done, it had proved that where there was goodwill and determination, then practical difficulties could be gradually overcome. Not only did the children sail out, but in the same ship went other passengers who had missed out on earlier chances to travel. In arranging for wives of convicts to sail out to New South Wales, Caroline had found a number of other convict relatives who also wanted to go − but they were male relatives and therefore could not travel on a ship which had been specifically arranged for women. The Home Secretary proved sympathetic to their plight, and they went on the *Sir Edward Parry*. This practical solution had been suggested by the Colonial Land and Emigration Commissioners. Mr T. Frederick Elliot and Mr C. Alexander Wood wrote to James Stephen at the Colonial Office saying that they 'by no means propose such a measure as a precedent, or proper in itself, but we merely submitted it as being the best course available, supposing the conveyance of these People was demanded by good faith'.[9]

Caroline could feel that, despite the disappointment over a number of the 'bounty children' who would not be reunited with their families, something great had been achieved. Attitudes were changing. The Colonial Office, the Home Office, and the Land and Emigration Commissioners, were beginning to respect the views and wishes of the settlers already in Australia, and not merely to see emigration from a bureaucratic point of view. Even though she had only been in London a few months, her work was well under way. Yet there remained much to be done.

## Notes

1. Public Record Office, ref CO 201; 390.
2. *The Tablet*, London April 10th 1847.
3. *The Sequel to Catholic Emancipation*, Mgr Bernard Ward, Longmans Green and Co, 1915.
4. Public Record Office, 201; 390.
5. Public Record Office, CO 201; 390.
6. Public Record Office, CO 386; 122.
7. ibid.
8. ibid.
9. Public Record Office, CO 654; page 151.

# Chapter Nine

# 'The Emigrant's Friend'

The Chisholms did not stay at Mile End – once they had improved their contacts in London they found more convenient accommodation in King Street, Covent Garden. Their house was number 38 and it was from here that Caroline carried out the bulk of her work over the next few months.[1]

She was very anxious to bring home not only to the Government authorities in Britain, but also to the wider British public, the realities of the Australian scene. For a long time, she had wanted to publish in Britain some of her first-hand accounts of settlers' stories. One of the first things she had done after establishing contact with both the Colonial Office and the Land and Emigration Commissioners, was to send them some of her papers which conveyed accurate and vivid information about conditions in Australia. She asked for advice on how to get this material published. In December 1846 Mr T.J. Elliot of the Commissioners wrote to her at Prince's Street: 'I am much obliged to you for letting me see these papers, and need not say that their contents are so very interesting to anyone who has any concern in Emigration. To the poor they would chiefly be important, in proportion to the means which might exist of satisfying the desire they would excite to emigrate; and these means are I regret to say, at present not very extensive. The question therefore of the expediency of publishing the papers is a very delicate one, on which I should feel a good deal of difficulty in offering an opinion, on account of the pain I have often seen the poor suffer from disappointment of hopes and wishes raised in their minds, before there are the means of giving them effect.'

But Caroline was not to be deflected from the idea of publication merely because of a bureaucratic brush-off. She had proved, through her efforts to secure passages for the convicts' wives and the bounty children, that it was possible to break down official resistance and even to turn it into willing support.

She knew that the only way to encourage interest in Australia was to tell the truth about what was happening there. Mr Elliot was right about poor people having their hopes raised with regard to emigration. But why not try to seek practical ways of bringing their hopes to fulfilment? A wave of public support for emigration, and changed Government attitudes towards it, would bring great benefits.

In 1847, therefore, two booklets appeared, both of which swept Emigration to the forefront of public debate. Caroline had decided to produce a detailed and considered document, designed for Government scrutiny, and a quite different popular booklet aimed at impoverished families seeking emigration as a solution to their problems.

*Comfort for the Poor! Meat Three Times a Day!* was the eye-catching title of the latter booklet. It was subtitled *Voluntary Information from the People of New South Wales collected in that colony 1845−6*, and it was packed with the same human stories that had already attracted interest when they were printed in Australia. Here they all were: the farmer giving details of his crops and sheep, the impoverished city girl transformed into a contented Australian wife. The stories told of loneliness and hard work, but also of well-spread tables, hams hanging up from kitchen rafters, wheat ripening in the sun. Caroline had wisely stuck to the idea of reproducing exactly what people said, taken down verbatim. It made lively reading, and people were gripped by it. Here indeed was comfort for Britain's poor. Caroline was careful to emphasise the importance of family links − large numbers of the statements from settlers made the point that they would like to send for their relatives to join them. Instead of shipping people out to an unknown future, emigration in the future would mean helping families to reunite in a country where prosperity had already been established.

The 'voluntary statements' also made up a great bulk of her other publication, which bore the more formal title *Emigration and Transportation relatively considered, in a*

*Letter dedicated by Permission to Earl Grey*. Here the settlers' testimonies were prefaced with a plea for a complete change of policy. Referring in her opening paragraphs to the 'unparalled misery and distress' that afflicted Britain, Caroline made a heartfelt cry for the poor:

'The system so long pursued of peopling Australia with prisoners, naturally raised strong prejudices against free emigration, and which nothing but the extraordinary success and prosperity of her people could have removed; but the period has now arrived when a free passage to these Colonies is eagerly sought for by honest men and respectable families ... Is it not a lamentable thought, then, my Lord, that deaths should daily result from starvation among British subjects, while in this valuable colony good wheat is rotting in the ground for the want of hands to gather it in − that tens of thousands of fine sheep, droves after droves, thousands upon thousands of fat cattle are annually slaughtered there and 'boiled down' in order to be rendered into tallow for the European market, while the vast refuse is cast into the fields to be devoured by dogs and pigs, and yet no effort is made by England to provide for her struggling people by a humane system of colonisation.'

Caroline was speaking in language which made it clear that moral issues were at stake: justice, fair play, and dignity for ordinary people. 'Let me then, in the name of suffering humanity, entreat of your Lordship to take into mature and immediate consideration, this demand for labour − this fearful waste of human food, and withal the vast capabilities of our Australasian Colonies (nearly equal in size to all of Europe); and let me hope that the result of your Lordship's deliberation and that of other friends of humanity, will be to give some of our starving peasantry a passage to a country admirably adapted to the hard-working man.'

In writing this, Caroline was in fact changing the public image of Australia in Britain for all time. As her booklet was distributed, sold, read, and re-read, it aroused debate and discussion everywhere. Its human stories provoked interest and its passion provoked feeling. Readers were moved by its patriotism and its conviction. They felt stirred by exciting tales of these distant colonies, angered at the waste of potential, and moved by the tales of human endeavour which had produced farms and food out of what had been regarded as a penal settlement on the very edge of the world.

From the time that the two booklets started to circulate can be traced a totally new view of Australia which began to pervade the public consciousness in Britain. The old image of a remote territory out on the terrifying fringes of any known map was replaced by an image of farms and sunshine, strong family bonds and fierce British loyalty, courage and hard work and optimism. It was the beginning of an image that was to become a part of common culture.

Caroline had struck a chord. With the arrival of a young Queen on Britain's throne, the dramatic changes in industry and agriculture, the breakthroughs in transport through the improvement of roads and the creation of railways, had come a fresh spirit of pride and patriotism in the nation. But it was tempered with a new social conscience. Lord Ashley was beginning what was to be a lifelong crusade to free children from the horrors of working in mines and mills and factories. There was a renewed dedication to the cause of education – new schools were opening all the time – and a great earnestness over the question of Britain's role in the world. With this had come a new concern for the poor. The famine in Ireland, and the continuing poverty in England, were seen as a reproach to a powerful and proud nation. It was recognised that these were moral issues which needed to be addressed as touching the soul and conscience of the country. Mrs Chisholm wrote in language that everyone could understand.

'Are wretched starving beings to die without an effort?' wrote Caroline, 'Are the ports of England to be closed against our own subjects and our own brethren in search of bread for their famished children? ... Oh! if England would but take advantage of her outlets – her Colonies – how much would be relieved, and how much crime would be prevented.'

The booklet attracted attention everywhere. 'This little pamphlet has already reached a third edition' *The Tablet* reported in August. 'Good men in all quarters are calling attention to it, and its humane writer, not only in the columns of the periodicals but in placards on the walls, and at the windows, and indeed its subject-matter is of such grave consequence that any effort made to disseminate its precepts and inculcate its principles may be considered as a good work.'

It turned Caroline into a public figure, and soon she was to be almost as well known in London as she had been in New South Wales. Throughout 1847 her workload increased. Both pamphlets had carried her King Street address, and invited people to contact her there. This address was also published by other journals which mentioned her work, and was passed around among people who had heard about her emigration work. People came to her door, and she never let anyone go away without being attended to − although sometimes they had to wait as a queue formed.

Each day also brought her fresh letters and enquiries from would-be emigrants, and she was engaged in constant correspondence with Earl Grey and with the Land and Emigration Commissioners. There was still obstruction to many of her plans. No matter how much she pleaded for more women to be helped to go out to Australia, there always seemed to be some reason why it was not possible for them to go. The Commissioners were not above twisting her own arguments against her.

Thus, in May, Mr Rogers and Mr Elliot, on behalf of the Commissioners, were writing to the Colonial Office: 'The Convicts' wives are sent out by Funds at the disposal of the Home Department, but as the Emigrants now proposed have no relation to Convicts, we presume that their passage could not be paid for out of monies voted by Parliament for Convict Services.

'We trust that in pointing out these difficulties, we may not appear insensible to the desirableness of supplying New South Wales with respectable women. We are fully aware of the importance of that object. But it is necessary that we should submit, that the single obstacle to its accomplishment is the want of Funds. This evidently cannot be met by considering in what particular vessels they shall embark. Whatever the kind of Ship in which they go, their conveyance must be paid for, and as soon as this end is provided for, there would be no difficulty whatever in finding them a suitable conveyance.

'We represented this to Mrs Chisholm, who appeared entirely to take the same view. Indeed, she went further, since even if a Colonial Fund were available, she doubted whether it could, at any rate in the outset, be appropriated to the present purpose. For highly important as are the moral grounds for wishing to send women of good character into the Colony, yet the urgent want to which the Colonists are anxious their resources should be devoted is the supply of labor; and if, after a suspension of Emigration for some years, the first use which was made of any Colonial Funds was to send out nothing but Female Emigrants, Mrs Chisholm fears that it would only excite discontent and complaints.'

It was extremely difficult to argue with these people, who too often seemed immune to human pleas for practical help. Caroline had suggested to the Commissioners that Parliament be urged to make a grant of money specifically available for sending out young women to Australia, 'on account of the injury which has been inflicted on the Colony by sending into it so large an excess of Males as Convicts'. But, the Commissioners concluded almost triumphantly 'We felt obliged to mention to Mrs Chisholm that we feared such a grant was not probable and we ourselves are not aware of any other means by which the plan can be carried into execution.'[2]

This particular correspondence had been started because of a request from Caroline to Earl Grey that some emigrants be allowed to travel to Australia on the ship carrying the bounty children. 'I am sure it will be quite unnecessary for me to advert to the evil consequences to Society which have ensued from the System which had been pursued of sending to the Colony such an overwhelming excess of male Prisoners' she wrote. 'The difficulty of procuring respectable females has hitherto been very great, may I therefore hope that the present favorable disposition may be promptly met. The numbers of Females whom I wish to introduce is 500, about one half of these I calculate upon would be received by their relations on their arrival in New South Wales and for the others I can even from here make arrangements for their being provided with respectable places of Service.'

It was irritating that stonewalling seemed to be the automatic response to many of her requests. It was always couched in polite langauge, but the effect was always the same. Problems which she felt could be overcome — such as the question of whether something was the responsibility of the Home Office (because it related to convicts' families) or the Commissioners (because it related to general emigration) — seemed to be an excuse for inaction rather than a challenge to be overcome.

It was only her own growing reputation with the public that began to achieve a change of attitude. The Commissioners still seemed to regard their task as that of merely managing — rather than promoting and encouraging — emigration. But Caroline's public efforts meant that the whole concept of emigration was changing. It was becoming a matter of discussion and enthusiasm at every level of society. The Commissioners' old-fashioned and staid approach was being challenged. Caroline was already seeing ahead to the formation of new organisations which would promote and develop emigration policies without having to fit into the strait-jacket of a Government department.

'I hope it may not be considered disrespectful to the Government my offering to do all I can to promote female Emigration gratuitously for I foresee much moral good may arise from it' she wrote to them. 'Many ladies are disposed to co-operate with me in a work of charity, who would object to connect themselves with paid Agency, and I feel that working for nothing will prevent a certain Class of Agents from offering their services who would not be very particular in their selection ...'[3]

Caroline had always preferred private initiative to cumbersome bureaucratic Government-funded action. Her Home in Sydney had flourished chiefly through private enterprise. Ordinary people rallied round to help, because it was a genuine response to an evident need. Surely the same sort of thinking was needed here in England? It was these ideas that were to lead her, over the next few years, to launch her own organisation, the Family Colonisation Loan Society. But in 1847 that still lay in the future.

Meanwhile she had at least been mobilising public opinion, by telling the truth about Australia and the great hope that it offered for the poor, and pointing to the scandalously inadequate policies that were preventing the poor from benefiting. In her pamphleteering, she had captured a public mood. The rapid improvement of communications — the postal system, the speedier movement of ships that was soon to improve with the arrival of steam power — brought a new urgency to the need to uncover public inefficiency and to demand action to right injustices. News travelled swiftly, and there was a new sense of urgency about tackling problems and facing up to particular challenges.

Although she had yet to make much headway with the authorities in charge of emigration, Caroline had built up a public following which was liable to create its own momentum. Without actually planning to do so, she had fostered, in effect, a political lobby for changes in emigration policy. The work had been frustratingly slow. London was wealthy, but little of the cash available for charitable work had seemed to flow her way. It was the most politically important city in the world, but she had found it hard work to get a hearing among the policy-makers.

Finally, the breakthrough came. In April and June of 1847 she was summoned to give evidence to two Parliamentary Select Committees. The first was the Select Committee on the Execution of the Criminal Law, which had started its work in 1845. The second was the Select Committee of the House of Lords appointed to enquire into Colonisation from Ireland, under the chairmanship of Lord Mounteagle of Brandon.

She was to find her experience of these Committees both exciting and frustrating. She was aware of the enormous importance of what might emerge from their work, but at times found that they were simply not asking the right questions.

Caroline went before members of the Select Committee on the Execution of the Criminal Law, on 20th April. From her point of view — that of changing the whole image of Australia and encouraging free emigration — it proved to be a rather unhelpful exercise. The Committee members were clearly most concerned to find out about the conditions under which convicts had been living in Australia, to investigate allegations of brutality and cruelty, and to seek evidence on which to base future penal policies. The discussion was not about emigration as such, but merely about the results and effects of transportation.

A verbatim account of the evidence given by Mrs Chisholm was printed in May. It was in fact most unusual for a woman to give evidence to a Select Committee in Parliament, but no one mentioned the fact that Mrs Chisholm might be making history, or creating a precedent for members of her sex.

'You have been in Australia, have you not?
Yes.
You were never at Van Dieman's Land, were you?
Only for a short Period.
How long were you in that Colony?
Upwards of Seven Years.
Had you in that Time the Opportunity of any Intercourse and Conversation with the Convicts?
Constantly.'

And so it went on, with Mrs Chisholm appearing rather reserved and evidently anxious not to seem too familiar. Perhaps she was a little overawed by her surroundings. She was also possibly a little too anxious to emphasise the blessings of life in Australia − in her desire to promote emigration and to show how good life in the colony could be, she was in danger of minimising the horrors of transportation. When asked about how convicts had felt on looking back on their days as prisoners before obtaining their 'ticket of leave' she simply said 'I think there is an unwillingness to speak of these things generally', and when pressed to give convicts' views on the subject of transportation she said 'They consider it a punishment; but I have not heard them express themselves very strongly upon that point.' While emphasising that convicts certainly looked back on Norfolk Island (the notorious convict prison on the coast near Sydney) as a punishment, she tried to turn the conversation in another direction. Her aim was to show the good side of life in Australia, and to stress that many former convicts had in fact gone on to settle in creative employment after serving their sentences.

This was perhaps not a very clever approach. It clearly baffled members of the Committee, who were left with the impression that, on Mrs Chisholm's evidence, transportation had not been such a bad idea after all. This clearly conflicted with all the other evidence they had received about the horrors of life on Norfolk Island, and the misery of men wrenched away from their families in England and sent abroad in squalid ships to serve out sentences under conditions of brutality. Because the Committee members did not have a clear picture of life in Australia, they must have felt very confused about just what was happening there. Was it a place of brutality and hopelessness, as much of the evidence presented to them had seemed to indicate, or did it in fact offer great opportunities for people who had not done well in Britain, as Mrs Chisholm appeared to be saying? The answer, of course, was that there were many aspects to life in Australia. Caroline had never been a supporter of transportation, and knew more than most people how much suffering it had caused. But in her eagerness to win support for better ideas for the future, she found herself unintentionally downplaying the miseries of Australia's convict past. It was a difficulty which was to face many other campaigners on Australia's behalf over the next century: how to promote an attractive image of the place for would-be emigrants while admitting the truth about the darker aspects of its heritage.

Caroline's next venture into the Houses of Parliament was a far happier one. On 12th June she was called to give evidence to the Committee looking at Colonisation from Ireland.

Here at last she was truly in her element. She knew that this was her opportunity to speak up for Ireland's hungry and poor, and to tell of the wonderful opportunities that Australia offered them. Right from the beginning, she spoke with confidence and spiced her answers with vivid accounts of her work. She was asked all about her Home in Sydney, and then about employment possibilities out in the Bush. Before long, she was reading to the Committee some of the statements she had collected from the people of New South Wales. In one dramatic moment, when she was asked about the quality of the wheat produced, she produced some from her handbag. The formal report of the proceedings noted it all down meticulously:

'You have seen arable Cultivation in the Colony?

Yes.

Is the Wheat of good Quality?

The Wheat is of very good Quality. I have brought a Sample which is Two Years old (producing the same). This is Wheat grown on the Farm of a man whose Statement I have just read. Twenty-five Bushels per Acre, and Sixty-Two Pounds and a Half the Bushel.'

When she read out the statements from the settlers in the bush, their forthright language and enthusiasm for their new way of life must have rung oddly in the formal committee chamber of the House of Lords. Caroline read one such statement from a tenant farmer who had arrived in Australia in 1839:

'I left Sydney on the 2nd of May, for the Service of Dr Bowman, Brother-in-Law to our present Landlord. He gave us weekly Thirteen Pounds of Flour, Twelve Pounds of Meat, and new Milk as we wanted it, and £20 a year for the Services of myself and Wife. I was a Farm Labourer, and my Wife was House Servant, but I did not allow my Wife to work the Second Year. I got £26 the Second Year, and Sixteen Pounds of Meat, Eighteen Pounds of Flour, and as much Milk as the Children and Ourselves required. We were well and regularly paid; had a good Master. I would sooner be on the farm than not. I have Forty Acres of Land on a Twenty-One year Lease by Mr McArthur's word; he is a Man that his Word does as well as a Bond. The First Year I paid no Rent, the Second 2s.6d [12p] an Acre, advancing at 2s.6d until it gets to 10s [50p] an acre, when it is to remain at that Price. The Land is very good, I grow Wheat and Corn ... This much I have got to say: I know I should never have got a Plough or a Set of Bullocks in England; not if I had worked my Eyes out of my Head; and yet I was a very hard-working Man there, and made a Living.'

Caroline also read a rather more formal and flowery letter from the Speaker of the House of Assembly in Sydney. But its message echoed that of the settlers' in its plea for more emigrants to come from Britain to enjoy the land:

'I address this Letter to you from Lake George, where I have been staying for a few Days. The Country generally is looking beautiful, and is covered with a Carpet of the richest and thickest Turf. On the Farms where Cultivation is carried on there are abundant Crops, and the Trees in the Orchards are bent to the Ground with Fruit. All these Gifts of Providence are in a great measure rendered valueless for want of Man to enjoy and partake of them. Farmers will not grow Wheat for want of a market, and in an Orchard in Goulbourn I was told that the choicest and most luxuriant Fruits with which the Trees were loaded would not be plucked, as they were not worth the Labour of pulling. All this Redundance of the Necessaries and Luxuries of Life is rendered valueless from the great and increasing Scarcity of Labour. Wages, since you left, have, I should say, nearly doubled. In many parts of the Colony Shepherds are receiving £30 and £40 a year ...'

There was also a letter from a woman settler, urging other members of her family to join her: 'Dear Brother, if you cannot come, do all you can to send out my Three Sisters, as we very much want them here, for it seems so hard to us to pay Strangers to live with us, when our own Sisters would be very comfortable here with us. I hope when they do come they will not ccme alone, but bring some of their Neighbours with them, for this Letter I hope will encourage a great many of them to come. I thank God most heartily myself for coming here, and if my sisters only knew how well Ellen is doing I am sure they would be glad to come, for I have no doubt they would do equally as well.'

Caroline urged that farms be 'thrown open' to emigrants, and was asked to explain the phrase. She said that she meant 'Making it easy for the poor Man when he has saved his Money to purchase a Farm without Loss of Time to himself; and that he should know where the Land is, that it should be surveyed.' She wanted people with small amounts of money to be able to buy land easily on the open market, through auctions, and not have to see it all bought up by richer people who could simply acquire huge property holdings by marking off areas on a map.

Caroline spoke warmly and enthusiastically about how the country people in Australia helped one another, and how committees in different areas throughout New South Wales had assisted her work. Describing how she had taken girls out into the bush to settle them with families, she explained the sort of support and encouragement she had been given: 'A Gentleman who was examined before your Lordships the other Day, Mr William Bradley, a Native of the Colony, called upon me, and told me that he approved of my Views, and that if I required anything in carrying my Country Plan into operation I might draw upon him for Money, Provisions, Horses, or indeed anything that I required. I had no necessity to draw upon him for a Sixpence, the People met my Efforts so readily; but it was a great Comfort for me at the Time to be thus supported.'

She gave the Committee examples of the contracts that were used in employing new settlers on farms, and also explained her own ideas for a society or organisation that would help people to emigrate. This was a subject close to her heart, and she and Archibald were already working out plans for it.

Perhaps the Committee knew of her reputation in Australia as a matchmaker, for she was specifically asked about the marriage prospects of young female settlers:

'Did you find that many of the Female Emigrants married?

Almost all of them. One of the most serious Impediments I met with in transacting Business in the Country was the Application made for Wives. Men came to me, and said "Do make it known in Sydney what miserable Men we are; do send wives to us." The Shepherds would leave their Sheep, and would come for Miles with the greatest Earnestness for the Purpose. I never did make a Match, and I used to tell them that I could not do anything of the Kind; but the Men used to say "I know that, Mrs Chishom, but it is quite right that you should know how very thankful we shall be" and they would offer to pay the Expense of Conveyance, etc. I merely mention this to show the Demand for Wives in the Interior.'

She added, in response to further questions, that she still maintained contact with many of the girls she had settled, and who had subsequently married, and that many had written to her begging her help in sending for their sisters and friends. 'Certainly I should not feel the Interest I do in Female Emigration if I did not look beyond providing Families with Female Servants – if I did not know how much they are required as Wives, and how much moral Good may be done in the Way.'

When Caroline left the House of Lords after the lengthy session before the Committee – in all she had answered 131 questions, many of them in great detail – she had every right to feel satisfied with her contribution. For the first time, the case for proper emigration had been set before a Parliamentary body, and a vision given of the possibilities of the future. It had been the climax of so much that she had returned to England from Australia to accomplish. In an important sense, it marked a watershed, because giving evidence to this Committee had established her as someone who spoke with specific authority in the field of emigration, and who possessed information and ideas that were of real value. From now on, she was recognised by the offical authorities, and not just by the ordinary people, as 'The Emigrant's Friend.'

**Notes**

1. The house still stands, but now has a shop front and is known as the Africa Centre. The road is now part of a largely pedestrianised Covent Garden redevelopment centred on the shops and restaurants of an area popular with tourists.
2. Correspondence in Public Record Office.
3. Ibid.
4. The full reports of these Committees were published in the usual way: Vol XXIII, 1847 of the Seasonal Papers of the House of Lords. I am grateful to Mr Bob Hughes, MP, for obtaining this material for me from the House of Commons library.

# Chapter Ten

# Islington

Although 1847 had been a very busy year for Caroline, her family was still the centre of her life. The house at King Street was very much a family home, dominated by children. Her visits to Parliament and to government offices were only made possible because of the presence of her mother as an active and enthusiastic grandmother, taking charge of the children while Caroline was out of the house.

By the end of the year Caroline knew that the family was going to increase further: another baby was expected. The four boys – Archie, William, Henry and Sydney – were now happily settled. They were used to a house where there was bustle and activity, and where the furniture and fittings were unpretentious and used to the knocks and scratches of everyday life. The Chisholms had no money to spare for luxuries, and the housekeeping had to be modest and frugal. A further suggestion had come from Australia that Caroline might receive an official grant for her work, but she had refused. She was keen to be seen as independent, and not as the lobbyist or agent for the colonial authorities, or for any particular sectional interest. She remained convinced that voluntary effort brought out the best in people: she now had a small team of helpers who assisted with the distribution of 'Comfort for the Poor!' and other tasks, and she could rely on their goodwill and high motives. In fact her decision on this, although it was to mean that the family suffered financial hardship, was wise. Throughout her years of public life, she was never accused of having any pecuniary interest in her efforts, and everyone knew that she worked simply out of a genuine desire to help poor emigrants. The modest lifestyle itself had practical advantages for the work: no one, however shabbily dressed, felt uncomfortable knocking at her door and going into her little office.

The new baby was born on May 13th 1848 at King Street: to their delight it was a little girl. They named her Caroline Monica. On the birth certificate, Archibald's occupation was given as 'gentleman' – although he used his Army rank of Captain he was living as a retired officer, and their only income was his pension.

The addition to the nursery meant that a more suitable home was needed. They found one further out in the suburbs, in Islington. It was number 3, Charlton Crescent, a four-storey terraced house fronting directly on to the street, not far from the main road. This part of London was growing fast. It teemed with life and bustle, and was an ideal centre from which to run a centre of information and assistance for families wanting information about Australia. Poverty mingled here with suburban respectability. Just down the street was an old-clothes shop where lived a character whom Charles Dickens would one day immortalise as the 'Artful Dodger'. Irish labourers who had settled in London had established a community for themselves which focused on a recently completed Catholic church – St John the Evangelist in Duncan Terrace. They mingled with people who ended up in Islington from many parts of Britain – lured to London by the hope of jobs or the chance of wider travel.

The convenience of having a Catholic church so near was probably a major factor in the decision of the Chisholms to settle in Charlton Crescent, and their choice of home turned out to be particularly happy because a couple of years later their friend Canon Oakley – who will feature further in the story – was to arrive at St John's as parish priest. Meanwhile they quickly became regular worshippers at the church. On July 18th the new baby was baptised there. Although she had been given her mother's name and confirmation name, it was clearly going to be confusing having two Carolines in the family. The baby was always to be 'Carry' and in fact it was this name and not the formal full version of her name that was entered in the parish baptismal register.

The baby kept Caroline happy and busy at home for most of 1848. She was perfectly sincere when she recommended to others the joys of domesticity − she enjoyed being a wife and mother even though she did it in circumstances that were far from luxurious. She was a good mother − her children would speak of her with affection all their lives, and the family was a united one.

The wider Chisholm links were not forgotten either. Archibald may have left behind the rural Scottish life of his childhood, but he remained proud of being a Chisholm and fond of his family. There was a trip north to see them all on a lengthy holiday, showing the new baby and the growing boys with pride.

Even when family life had to take priority over campaigning work, however, the results of earlier efforts were being felt and brought more work with them. The long hours spent in tracing lost relatives of convicts and other settlers had resulted in many families being reunited on Australian soil. During 1847, in addition to the sailing of the *Sir Edward Parry* and the *Asia* there had been passages arranged through Caroline on other ships for larger numbers of people. Now she began to hear of the safe arrival of these new emigrants − and every success story brought renewed requests for help for others.

The letters that arrived from happily settled emigrants in Australia, wanting to send for their families and friends, did not gather dust on Caroline's desk. In addition to giving them all the practical help she could, she was planning a major venture which would tackle the problem in the future. She and Archie planned to set up their own emigration society. This would mean freedom from the restrictions and injustices of the Government schemes, and would focus on free enterprise and family links as the main means of enabling people to get to Australia. It would be a society run for and by people who really had the cause of Australia at heart.

During 1848 and 1849 Caroline made her contacts and laid her plans. A priority was to establish a committee of influential people who would give the society the status it needed, and help with the all-important task of raising funds. The idea was that families would pay as much as they could towards their own passage to Australia, but that this would be 'topped up' by loans from the society, which in turn would be paid back once the settlers had established themselves.

Since Caroline was by now well known as Australia's champion, it was not difficult to make links with people who admired what she was trying to do and wanted to help. She had also to work out the financial aspects of the new society's work.

Already, emigration had changed radically in the time that Caroline had been campaigning. The tragedy in Ireland was responsible for much of the new pressure to emigrate, of course, but it was Caroline who urged the importance of allowing and encouraging families to emigrate together, and of seeing women and children not as 'encumbrances' but as people with their own rights, who would be a blessing to the new land. But through her own emigration society she would be able to put these ideas into practice and not merely have to lobby on the sidelines.

The person who would be of most help to Caroline during the earliest stages of creating this new organisation was Lord Ashley, the prominent Evangelical Tory Member of Parliament. He was known for his work for the poor, which ranged from the establishment of 'ragged schools' to crusading against child slave labour in mines and factories. As the heir to the Earl of Shaftesbury, he might have had a life of ease and comfort, but his Christian faith and social conscience had shown him another way.

After prolonged discussions and negotiations with him, Caroline was finally able to launch her Family Colonisation Loan Society publicly with a pamphlet addressed to him. It was a clever move. The whole idea of emigration as a source of hope for the poor was swept into the headlines.

'FAMILY COLONIZATION LOAN SOCIETY
by a grant of loans for Two Years or more without interest
OR
A SYSTEM OF EMIGRATION
TO THE COLONIES
Of
NEW SOUTH WALES, PORT PHILLIP and SOUTH AUSTRALIA
In a Letter

Dedicated by Permission to Lord Ashley, MP
by Mrs Chisholm.'²

read the front of the pamphlet, and the reader's attention was
secured for another of Mrs Chisholm's impassioned pleas for
the poor, this time offering a practical means by which they
would be able to help themselves out of their misery. It was
to prove her best idea yet.

'It is indeed melancholy to reflect, that thousands of British
subjects should wander about more like spectres than beings of
flesh and blood, and that hundreds should die from starvation
while our vast Colonies could provide so abundantly for them.
Anxious, however, as a poor man may be to emigrate to the
Australian Colonies with his family, it is unfortunately impossible for him to accomplish his desire without some assistance'.
The pamphlet made it clear that this assistance was now to be
forthcoming. Well-to-do people would be invited to donate
money enabling poor people to emigrate − and the poor would
also be shown how to help themselves. They would be able to
apply for loans which would pay their fares to Australia, and
then pay back the money once they had prospered in the new
colony. But there was more. The would-be emigrants would
meet together, forming small groups who would make the
long sea journey together and help one another in all the
necessary arrangements. Emigration would become a family
venture as well as a great national enterprise. Caroline's Open
Letter to Lord Ashley was to prove the rallying-call for a great
crusade − a call which found an echo in many people's hearts.
It offered a practical way in which poor families could find a
whole new way of life, and it brought together people who,
alone and frightened, might never have found a way out of
their difficulties.

A Committee was established to get the Society off the
ground. It included, of course, Lord Ashley, and also the
Member of Parliament for Caroline's own old home of Northampton, Mr Vernon Smith. Northampton was beginning to feel
proud of this local daughter whose fame was steadily spreading
and whose open commitment to the values of a hard-working,
family-based way of life reflected well on the town. Another
prominent MP on the Committee was the Rt Hon. Sidney

Herbert. He was to prove active in the cause of emigration, but it was his wife who really threw herself into it with total dedication. She had for some while been deeply concerned about the plight of destitute young women who attempted to earn money by doing sewing. They were grossly exploited and overworked. It had recently been discovered that some were paid as little as 1½d for making a shirt – a task involving hours of hand-stitching and delicate, careful work. Elizabeth Barrett Browning, who was becoming a well known poet, had written dramatically about them in 'The Song of the Shirt'. Mrs Herbert saw that many of them would like to emigrate and find a better life for themselves, and she willingly teamed up with the Chisholms to see how this could be done.

Caroline was still steadfastly refusing to accept any salary for her work. The Society arranged that a modest fund was available for basic office expenses – postage was a particular burden with a large stack of mail arriving and departing each day from Islington. Everything was to be done as cheaply as possible, and from the start, the strength of the Society was that its operation was straightforward and simple. People would pay one shilling to join, and then be helped and encouraged to save for their fares to Australia while obtaining a loan to cover the remainder of the sum needed. When the loan was repaid, a further sum of ten shillings for every adult in the family and five for every child was payable. This had been agreed as being simpler and easier to administer than a system of working out interest on the loans.

Just as Caroline had created a legend in Australia when she set out on her white horse to lead waggon-trains of emigrants into the bush, so she now created a different kind of legend here in London. As dusk gathered on an evening appointed for one of her emigrants' group meetings, groups of people would be seen making their way to the house in Charlton Crescent. Welcomed at the door and ushered in, they would find themselves seats on the rows of benches in a simply-furnished room and hear a short talk on the practicalities of emigration from Mrs Chisholm. She did not preach at them, or theorise about the concept of emigration either – her talks were entirely practical. Listeners would hear what a typical cabin looked like on board ship with its bunk beds, what items were needed for the voyage, how to cope with a small baby, the importance of cleanliness and the wisdom of making plans in advance for entertainment and instruction during what might otherwise be tedious days. Caroline knew the concerns and fears of potential emigrants at first-hand. When she spoke about the long sea voyage, and about the land that awaited the newcomers at the other end, she was speaking from personal experience. These evenings were, for many people, their first introduction to a great family adventure.

When a family first enquired about possible emigration, Caroline helped them to work out plans and showed them how to budget so that a suitable loan could be arranged. If they decided to make the big decision and go ahead, they became part of a friendly network which would link them up with others making their way to the new land. They would arrive for an evening session and, after hearing the initial talk from Caroline, would find themselves allocated to a small group. This group would be the one with which they would travel to Australia. Single girls and young men were put in the care of families. This was an innovation, and it was a guarantee that there would be no more terrified young people struggling alone during a long sea voyage, subjected to humiliation and sexual and other abuse while unable to escape. Usually, a young girl would be put in the care of a family that had a daughter of the same age: the two would get to know one another during the evening meetings and by the time the voyage came would have shared ideas and plans as well as practical arrangements over such things as luggage and the daily timetable for shipboard life.

People remembered these Islington evenings long afterwards. There would be Caroline's quiet, measured voice reading aloud from letters that had just arrived from Australia, giving the latest news from the colony and starting a discussion on jobs and farming prospects. There would be the display of useful items: a tin mug, other shipboard utensils and suitable clothing. There would be answers to general questions about the voyage or about formalities on arrival. Then there would be the eager chat once the groups formed, the mutual sharing of ideas for making or mending items needed for the trip, the sense of solidarity in preparing for a life-changing experience.

Most of the emigrants already had family members out in Australia — a major part of these evening meetings consisted of the sharing of news from recent letters. The mood was friendly and cheerful. Sometimes another Committee member of the Society would give a short address.

Caroline played a very active part in all of this as the Society took shape, but in the last weeks of 1849 she had to retire from the scene for a while. Another baby was now expected, and was duly born in January: a little girl, who was baptised Sara Monica at St John the Evangelist Church. The baptism took place on January 30th.

Always, Caroline's concern for the welfare of other people's families found its essential inspiration in the love and joy she found in her own family circle. In a family that had started with boys, it was a special joy to welcome another little girl, who would be a sister to Carry, now a toddler. But the joy was not to last long. Baby Sara did not have the robust health of her older brothers and sister. In August 1850, at the age of only six months, she died of a throat infection.

If was an age when families were large and infant death not uncommon, but such babies still did not die unmourned. For both Caroline and Archibald, the effect of the experience was to create a greater understanding of the sorrow that is part of family life, and to renew their efforts to ensure that anyone in any distress or difficulty was treated with special consideration.

Work filled the void created by the baby's loss. It was not enough simply to found an emigration society: a ship must be chartered and the standard of its accommodation ensured. Later on, Caroline would be famous for her crusades about shipboard health and for her lobbying for more effective regulations concerning access to fresh air and decent lavatories for all passengers. Meanwhile, the *Slains Castle*, chartered by the Society, was completely refitted to decent Chisholm standards. Out went all that belonged to the old days of dirt and overcrowding. In came family cabins to give complete privacy to married couples, and larger cabins to take groups of girls or boys. Neat bunks could be turned into seats for day-time use. There was provision for washing and for the preparation of food. A detailed list of regulations was drawn up, dividing all the passengers into two groups who would eat at separate times so as to avoid all confusion, and banning alcoholic drink and firearms. There were also strict rules about the use of lamps (a terrible fire hazard) and about the issuing of rations: a set amount of food was allowed per person for the voyage to ensure an adequate diet which was as varied and nourishing as circumstances would allow.

The ship captured the public imagination. Here at last was a voyage to Australia which was beginning with optimism and hope rather than with squalor and despair. Emigrants who were now veterans of several Islington meetings and committed members of their various small groups started to be allocated their cabins. The ship would be sailing with its full complement of passengers, and interest generated by the voyage was already starting to attract more would-be emigrants to the Society. Once this voyage was under way, it would be time to open the books for new members and charter another vessel.

Already, emigrants were becoming known as 'Mrs Chisholm's Children' and certainly many did look upon her as a sort of mother-figure. She was the source of information on every aspect of Australian life, and the person who could give straightforward answers to every question, however delicate or awkward, about the voyage. She spoke openly about family needs concerning water, food, and accommodation, and knew how to treat tactfully the enquiries of the poor and ill-educated who wanted the best for their children and elderly relatives but were not always able to express themselves well. Under her direction the *Slains Castle* became a vessel of which all associated with the Family Colonisation Society could be proud. It attracted much attention among the wider public, too − people were allowed on board to view the ship as it lay at anchor in the London docks, and to marvel at its conveniences.

The ship was due to sail at the end of September, just two months after baby Sara's death. A great meeting and rally was planned by the Committee of the Family Colonisation Loan Society to mark the event: all the emigrants and their families and friends would attend. This proved to be a memorable and emotional occasion. The Royal British Institution, in Tabernacle Row, just off the City Road, was booked for the evening. Banners decked the hall, including one specially made by some ladies who had embroidered Caroline's initials on to a blue background together with the name of the Society, and presented it to the Committee. Caroline was cheered to the echo as she took her seat on the platform, along with a groups of distinguished people − Committee members and supporters of the Society − who were to speak. It was a moment of triumph. All her ideas on emigration were summed up in what had been achieved on the *Slains Castle*. Families were travelling together, along with the single women that Australia so desperately needed to provide wives for the lonely men who had such good homes to offer them. The emigrants were travelling as friends, committed to work together and help one another. No one among them was a pauper: all had paid something towards the costs of the voyage and travelled with a sense of self-respect and in the knowledge that they had the backing of an organisation which trusted them and wished them well. Even the details mattered: one of Caroline's suggestions to her emigrant groups was that those who could not read and write might usefully learn during the voyage, and thus pass the time profitably. Religious sensitivities had been protected by rules which forbade proselytising on board ship. The day that the vessel sailed, there would be an Anglican service on the deck, and prayers led for the other denominational groups by their own ministers.

Mr Robert Lowe, from New South Wales, was a popular speaker at the meeting, and formally proposed the vote of thanks on behalf of all the emigrants to the Chisholm family. In his speech he struck a note of fiery patriotism as he emphasised the strong links that bound together England and Australia. It was a theme to which Caroline herself would often refer in speeches and echoed her own robust sentiments. Mr Vernon Smith also spoke, ending with a hearty 'God speed and farewell' on behalf of the Committee to all the travellers. Mr Wyndham Harding explained how the Society had operated and asked for further donations to enable a second ship to follow the *Slains Castle* as soon as possible. Only £600 was needed to make this possible: emigrants by their own efforts and through the generosity of benefactors had already raised the rest of the amount necessary.[3]

Caroline must have been moved and warmed by the three cheers that rang out for her at Mr Harding's bidding as the meeting drew to its close. Over the next couple of days, members of the public thronged the decks of the *Slains Castle* and peered into such of the cabins as were open to view. And then the time came for the vessel to sail. First, it went from London to Gravesend, with Caroline on board. As the ship left London, the emigrants had to make their final break with home. It was a scene which would be depicted in paintings and engravings, remembered for years by all those involved, described touchingly in letters, and written into folklore: the tears and flags, the blessings and greetings, the attempts at formality, and promises of letters and remembrances.

Caroline used the journey to Gravesend to make a continuous round of the ship, checking on details, answering enquiries, helping with small babies or tactfully showing sympathy with tearful passengers still weeping after a farewell to old friends. At Gravesend there was an overnight stop, and preparations were made for the final goodbyes. On the Sunday morning crowds gathered for the religious services. Over twenty clergymen took part in an Anglican service on the main deck, leading hymns and prayers in the open air. A Methodist minister then preached to members of his own denomination, and Catholics went to hear talks from two priests (it was not practical to try to arrange for Mass to be said on board). During the afternoon once again crowds of fascinated visitors poured over the ship, and then the next morning Caroline came on board for the last time to gather everyone together and give them her final messages. Many of the emigrants were weeping as they shook her hand or embraced her and stammered out their gratitude. She reminded everyone of the promises they had made to help one another, and especially of the commitment made by the men who as heads of families had offered protection to the young unmarried people in their care. Practical as ever, she spoke about the importance of using the long journey wisely, making use of the time to study or learn some new skill. She also reminded everyone of the need to protect religious liberty and ensure toleration during the voyage. It was a dramatic moment as she finally extricated herself and made her way ashore. The first group of 'Mrs Chisholm's children' was sailing off to the land to which she had directed them.


## Notes

1. The road's name was changed in 1922 to Charlton Place. The house is now marked with a blue plaque.
2. Published August 1849, London.
3. *Memoirs of Mrs Caroline Chisholm*, London 1842.

# Chapter Eleven

# A Grateful Nation

The middle years of the nineteenth century were a time of great change, and for many people, of great hardship. The rapid growth of cities following the Industrial Revolution brought thousands of men and women to places like London, Bristol, Birmingham and Manchester to work in the factories which sprang up to exploit the use of steam and mechanical power.

In Islington, Caroline was at the heart of this new city life. How much Britain had changed since her own Northamptonshire childhood. The big changes had been the arrival of cotton mills and the means of mass production in factories. Next, the growth of communications not only by rail but also by canal and on the new metalled roads. More and more raw materials were arriving, too, from overseas colonies, to be turned into household goods, clothing, or industrial equipment, and then re-exported.

For many, however, the welfare of mankind had to be remembered and nurtured at the centre of this change. Caroline's thinking on this echoed that of others. There was a stirring of social conscience beginning to emerge: a strong sense of the need to help the poor, and to speak up for the rights of people who were exploited as cheap labour.

Three people in particular were to emerge from this period of British history to become household names. Florence Nightingale whose dramatic innovations helped to establish nursing as a credible profession, Charles Dickens whose novels became classics, and Lord Ashley, later Lord Shaftesbury. On each of these three people Caroline was to have an influence which had lasting consequences.

Charles Dickens had met Caroline in the early months of 1850, not long after the birth of baby Sara. The introduction came via Mrs Sydney Herbert, who was an admirer of his work. When Dickens came to call at Charlton Crescent, the downstairs rooms were just in the process of being adapted so as to be used for meetings of emigrants, and fitted out with display-stands showing shipboard cooking utensils and other items relevant to the long voyage to Australia. Things were also busy at the house next door, which had just been acquired by the Society for use as an Emigrants' Home − a place where people could stay for the last few days before setting sail, after travelling from other parts of the country. Perhaps it was all this − plus the general sense of bustle usual in any young family − that made him comment afterwards on the poor standards of housekeeping! Nevertheless, he was to become a great friend to the cause of emigration, and to give Caroline the most important practical help he could − publicity. After hearing from her about what her Society was trying to do, he recognised that this was a scheme with which he heartily concurred, and one which, without being remotely patronising or sneering, really gave vital help to the poor. He saw too the great human drama being played out with the departure of each emigrant ship and with the arrival of each batch of letters from the colonies. As he soaked in all the information, he was storing it up for use in books and articles. Some of the Australian letters that Caroline showed to Dickens eventually reappeared in various forms in the magazine he edited. More memorably, a most vivid description of the departure of an emigrant ship was to appear towards the end of *David Copperfield*.

No one reading that account − the great dark ship against the sunset, the figure of Mr Peggoty among the emigrants on deck, with little Em'ly by his side − could doubt that it was written by someone who had grasped the full significance of what emigration entailed. Dickens could also portray the message with humour: the Micawber family, always waiting for 'something to turn up' while living in debt in England, were destined for fame and fortune in Australia. It was Charles Dickens, perhaps more than anyone, who showed to large numbers of people what emigration to Australia could mean − the great wrench that it involved in parting from England, but the great hope that it offered in a land of sunshine and opportunity. It is to an afternoon's conversation with Caroline

Chisholm in her unimpressive and probably rather untidy room in Charlton Crescent, with children scurrying in and out, that we owe a central part of the plot of *David Copperfield*, and the image that it indelibly printed on the minds of thousands of Australia as the place of refuge and fresh beginnings.

Dickens' own childhood had been marked by poverty, debt and sorrow. He had had to work in a blacking factory while his father languished in a debtors' prison, and he never forgot it. Perhaps, as he listened to Caroline talking about the practicalities of emigration, and describing how various families had made the successful transition from poverty at home to prosperity in the colonies, he thought back to his own home life. If his own father had emigrated, maybe the family might have followed the pattern, and made good? When, in *David Copperfield*, he created the character of Mr Micawber, he was writing with more than a hint of a memory of his own father. Mr Micawber, however, did not finish his days in debt and misery: he emigrated with his whole family to Australia and ended up as a leading citizen in a colonial community, honoured by a public dinner crowning a career of success and reported in newspapers shipped back to England. Caroline touched a chord in Dickens, and created in his mind a vision of Australia which was to echo and re-echo throughout his writings.

On the other hand, Dickens could not help being amused by Caroline's rather unusual domestic arrangements. Here was a mother with several children, who seemed oblivious to all the social conventions which dictated that she should be primarily attentive to their needs and to those of her husband. He was intrigued to know how they survived. Who was in charge of the domestic arrangements, while the lady of the house was absorbed in her colonial campaigning? Who looked after the children and saw to their education, the development of their social graces, their general health and well-being?

Dickens must have been a trifle baffled by Caroline Chisholm. She was neither a gentle Dora Spenlow nor an eccentric Betsy Trotwood. Later, he created a cruel caricature of a campaigning female in Mrs Jellaby, whose enthusiasm for the plight of natives abroad is contrasted with her contempt for any civilised life in her own home. To see a specific picture of Caroline here is inaccurate and absurd – but something of Dickens' bafflement at how Caroline coped, and amusement at the idea of a lady with a large family and a large campaigning organisation all squashed into one modest-sized Islington terraced house, is there in the creation of this character.

If Caroline influenced Dickens through personal contact, her influence on Florence Nightingale was the more remarkable because the two – at least as far as is known – did not actually meet. Miss Nightingale was to find her great moment of opportunity in the Crimean War – but it was in the years leading up to the war, when she was struggling to train as a nurse and begging to be allowed to play some active role in society, that she was affected by Caroline. The name of Mrs Chisholm was, during these years, beginning to be synonymous with a female capacity for achievement and worthwhile activity. Without ever meaning to do so, Caroline was giving encouragement and hope to others. Florence Nightingale was clearly inspired by her. As she fought with her family to be allowed to develop her plans for nursing the sick, she emphasised that all that she sought was an opportunity to be useful, and she mentioned specifically the name of Mrs Chisholm – along with that of Elizabeth Fry, the great prison reformer – as showing how a woman could work with dignity. In reply, her mother pointed out one major difference between Caroline and Florence – Mrs Chisholm was married and had a husband to protect and help her. The point, however, had been taken. Caroline's venture into public life was indeed opening the door for other women, and in this respect she was a major figure in changing the lot of nineteenth-century British women.

Lord Ashley was to be a major figure in Caroline's life and one with whom she was to work closely. They came from different backgrounds – she the farmer's daughter and he the eldest son of a peer – and there was an even greater difference in their religious views. Both were devout Christians, but Ashley belonged to the staunchly Evangelical wing of the Church of England, and sincerely believed Catholics to be deeply in error if not actually idol-worshippers. Caroline, as a Catholic convert, belonged to a category of people whose spiritual journey must have caused him some distress. Yet they were able to work together extremely effectively for the good of the poor. Ashley had long interested himself in their cause. He would eventually win a place in history-books as the man responsible for bringing before the nation the appalling plight of little children forced to work in mines, mills and factories. It was his efforts − and they were lifelong − that eventually brought laws banning such labour and opening the way for children to be given the right to protection from exploitation and the opportunity to go to school. But his concern for the poor extended beyond the conditions of their labour, and he saw in emigration a practical means of escape from the cycle of deprivation being endured by so many. In accepting a position on the Committee of Caroline's Society he immediately gave it the status it needed and assured it a reasonable flow of funds from people who trusted his judgement. He and Caroline would speak together at rallies, exchange friendly correspondence, and work well together at Committee meetings over a long period.

The year 1850 was one which as in fact to have huge significance for all Catholics in Britain. It had been decided in Rome that a full hierarchy of bishops should be restored to England, the country which for such a long time had been administered as 'mission territory'. The letter announcing the news came from Cardinal Wiseman, who was to become Archbishop of Westminster. Writing from Rome, he enthusiastically addressed and dated his letter 'from out the Flaminian Gate', and allowed himself to wax lyrical about the reclamation of the nation's heritage. He referred to 'Catholic England' being 'restored to its orbit in the ecclesiastical firmament' in language perhaps a little exaggerated. Fears, prejudices and passions were aroused. The Roman Church seemed to many to be announcing an impertinent attempt at a takeover bid, asserting its claims over the ancient dioceses of Canterbury and York and announcing to the world that the Anglican Church was no more. This was a distortion − all that Cardinal Wiseman had sought to do was establish an internal structure for the Catholic community of the country, with no pretensions to take over all that had long been in the hands of the Anglicans. But in the interval before he was able sufficiently to explain this, much damage was done.

The Prime Minister, Lord John Russell, rushed into print with a letter of his own, denouncing the Catholic Church's impertinence at claiming authority over England. Rioting broke out in streets where 'No Popery' became a convenient slogan for mayhem among people who had little idea of the real issues involved. Catholic churches were attacked and had their windows broken, and priests were pelted with stones. Elsewhere people attended public meetings to hear speakers denounce the 'Papal Aggression', and committees were set up to launch petitions and crusades in defence of the Protestant establishment.

An Ecclesiastical Titles Bill was put before Parliament by Russell, which would ban any Catholic bishop from assuming the title already used by an Anglican one. In a mood of hysteria, newspapers cartooned Catholicism, mocking its ceremonies and caricaturing some of its leading figures – notably Wiseman himself and the great convert of the day, John Henry Newman, who had recently left the Anglican Church and established a religious community, the Oratory, in Birmingham.

It was a testing time in which to be a Catholic public figure. Courage and level-headedness were needed, and fortunately Caroline had both. She had always taken care that her work was strictly non-sectarian. She never alluded to her religion in public, except when necessary to plead for the cause of tolerance as it affected emigration policy. Always, Caroline strove to show that her own faith in God was part of something that all should hold in common, and she was fond of using expression like 'God's providence' and references to His 'fatherly concern' which emphasised the universality and breadth of belief in Him. The cause of emigration was, she felt, in a profound sense God's work, but she had never seen it as remotely connected with Catholic missionary effort. It was simply a practical charitable project, making the blessings of God's providence available to all in need.

The rioting eventually died down and the subject retreated from public attention. Cardinal Wiseman wrote to the Prime Minister explaining that no territorial claim had been sought, and that all that was happening was a change of name and status within the internal structures of the church. He went further and made the point that in taking the title of

'Archbishop of Westminster' he sought no role whatever in the Parliament which met at Westminster, but merely wanted to work among the poorest of the people who lived within the city. This probably hit home – within yards of the great Palace of Westminster were some grim slums where there were many who needed the consolation and practical support of an active Christian Church.

Caroline, and other Catholics in public life, although subjected to various insults and embarrassments because of their beliefs – or what people imagined to be their beliefs – found that they were able to continue their work in peace once the immediate controversy had died down. In the end, greater problems were generally faced by people who were active Anglicans but who were felt to have 'Romanising tendencies', including many High Church clergymen. It was a debate which was to continue for many years.

A small, but significant number of Anglican clergymen had actually gone further and converted to Catholicism during the 1840s. One of these was the Revd Frederick Oakley, who eventually became a Catholic priest and a Canon. In 1850 he was appointed to the Islington parish where the Chisholms lived. They had known him before, when he had been among the clergy working at St George's church on the south bank of the Thames.

Canon Oakley was in his late fifties when he moved to Islington. He was to become well known as a hymn writer and translator – it was he who put the carol 'Adeste Fideles' into English: 'O come, all ye faithful'. Another of his hymns, sung each November, was in honour of St Andrew – perhaps a devotion fostered by his friendship with the Scottish Archibald Chisholm:

> 'Loved St Andrew, Scotland's patron,
> Watch thy land with heedful eye
> Rally round the Cross of Jesus
> All her storied chivalry!'

He translated a 13th-century hymn by St Bonaventure, 'In Passione Domini', and with others he wrote a hymn which has proved consistently popular for weddings, school assemblies and ecumenical occasions. It reflected Caroline Chisholm's own strong understanding of God as Father, protector, and provider:

> 'Praise we our God with joy
> And gladness never ending
> Angels and saints with us
> Their grateful voices blending
> He is our Father dear
> O'er filled with parent's love
> Mercies unsought, unknown
> He showers from above.'

For those sincerely trying to do Christian work, sacrifice is often necessary. Never shirking this, Caroline and Archibald faced the growing problem of how to manage the Australian end of things following the successful launch of the Family Colonisation Society (the word 'Loan' had been dropped from the Society's official name after a while, for brevity's sake). It was essential to have someone in Sydney who would manage the repayment of loans and help with general enquiries, promoting emigration by helping people to send for their relatives. No one came forward who was both prepared to take on the work and capable of doing it. Eventually it became clear that Archibald would have to take it on himself. So the decision was made that he would go to Australia, and establish an office there, sending for Caroline and the children as soon as it became possible to do so.

This would mean another long separation. Caroline and Archibald were no strangers to this idea, of course – indeed their whole married life had consisted of long periods of being apart from one another, punctuated by stretches of domesticity. There had been the long wait before Caroline could go out to India, right at the start of their marriage, and then the years in Australia after he had returned to duty in India. This new separation, however, had a sadder quality, partly because it was self-inflicted rather than dictated by the Army, and partly because it was coming after such a memorable time together in London, a time of achievement and work that had been shared with a growing family.

The decision was a hard one, and only made because it carried with it the bright prospect of a new chapter of life together in Australia. Archibald would work to establish a base from which they would create a new home there. They could look forward to raising the children in a colony which had prospered and flourished in the years since they had last seen it, and which held happy memories for them both and the lure of a bright future.

The preparations for Archibald's journey, and for the work he would do on his arrival, were extensive. He would be carrying the hopes and plans of many people with him. Establishing a sound base for the Family Colonisation Society in Australia would mean that the whole concept of family migration had finally come of age. It was important to see it done well. Whilst this goal and all the preparations for his voyage were exciting, it was with great sadness, however, that Caroline and Archibald finally said goodbye when he sailed in March 1851. There was an extra reason for their emotion. Another baby was now expected. Archibald would be far away in Australia when his child was born and it would be many weeks before he even knew if it was a boy or a girl and whether Caroline was well and the baby thriving.

Caroline's good health and natural sense of optimism and courage kept her going during the difficult weeks after her husband's departure. As always in her pregnancies, she was able to keep active and busy until quite near the time of the child's birth. Her mother was as always a source of strength and support.

The baby, Harriet Monica − always to be known by her second name − was born in July, the same month that her father arrived in Australia. Christened at St John's church, she was to be the last of Caroline's children, and the one who remained with her mother as the older ones were growing up and going their own way. The first departure came in fact not long after her birth, when William, the second boy, left to study in Rome. He hoped to become a priest, and followed the long tradition of boys from English Catholic families going abroad to train. He entered the Propaganda College in November 1851.

The family in Charlton Crescent continued, however, to be busy with the work of the Family Colonisation Society: while Caroline's mother, Mrs Jones, supervised the children, meetings of prospective emigrants still took place downstairs, and plans went ahead to fill more ships now that the *Slains Castle* had safely docked in Australia. The *Blundell* was the next to go, and with it came renewed interest in emigration, and further calls for Caroline to speak at meetings and rallies in other parts of Britain. She no longer had to plead in favour of emigration: instead, the need now was to ensure that the practicalities were tackled efficiently. She spoke out for decent shipping: enough space and air for all passengers, adequate cabins, proper lavatories and washrooms, access to the decks for necessary exercise. She also encouraged a sense of independence and initiative among all would-be emigrants, giving lectures on the sort of clothes and shoes they would need both for the journey and for life in rural Australia, and explaining how the loan system worked so that people would have a full understanding of their financial obligations and of the possibilities open to them through the Society.

Meanwhile news had arrived from Australia which was to change that country's reputation everywhere, and send men flocking there from all over the world: the discovery of gold. In fact, the first discovery of gold in New South Wales had occurred as far back as 1823. But the news was kept secret at an official level, for fear of what a gold rush would do to the colony. It is said that when Governor Gipps was shown a specimen of gold by a clergyman geologist who had found it at a remote site in the bush he said sharply 'Put it away, Mr Clarke, or we shall all have our throats cut!' The aim at that time was to encourage the peaceful and efficient rearing of sheep — the idea of people hurring to make a rapid fortune at the gold diggings was one which filled the authorities with horror.

In 1851, however, the news was no longer kept secret. Gold had been discovered in California, and men started to leave Australia to seek their fortunes there. A mild panic rippled through government circles in New South Wales. How could the colony retain its young men if the lure of gold was taking them to cram every ship leaving Sydney harbour for

America? So the news was released – Australia had goldfields of her own.

The flow to California slowed down and then ceased. Instead, men were soon heading for Australia's own gold fields. They left bush farms or jobs in Sydney or Melbourne, often abandoning their wives and children, convinced that they would soon return to them laden with wealth. When news of the gold spread to Britain, the reaction was the same. The gold rush was on.

In the face of this new enthusiasm Caroline went on steadily promoting and organising her own concept of family emigration – but with a renewed sense of urgency and a deep conviction of the need for people to see things in the right scale of priorities. The number of people who found instant fortunes in the gold-fields was very, very small. A far larger number found only disappointment, drunkenness, and the destruction of hopes.

The cause of family emigration was one which was steadily taking hold. Caroline was invited to speak at one major city after another, crossing to Ireland to speak at Dublin and at Cork, and travelling up and down England to speak at places as far apart as Birmingham and Southampton. Her lobbying for better conditions on ships was now something of a crusade. She urged all passengers to demand ventilation, lavatories, washrooms, and special hospital accommodation for the sick. She was instrumental in achieving a new Passenger Act in Parliament which ensured certain minimum standards. Her advice and opinion was sought because she was known to speak with real authority. In addition to lobbying at a political level, and addressing large rallies and public meetings, she continued to answer hundreds of personal letters. It was from these that she kept in close contact with the achievements, successes, and problems of emigrants once they had arrived in Australia. Many wrote asking her help in sending for relatives and friends. Large numbers simply wanted her to spread the news of the good life they had found – the sunny climate, the abundance of food, the willingness of settlers to help one another. She loved to read aloud extracts both at the small group meetings which continued at Charlton Crescent and at the bigger rallies.

Archibald had now settled in Melbourne, and was tackling the Australian end of the Family Colonisation Society with efficiency and care – and with a great deal of hard work. On his dedication and aptitude depended the reputation of the Society. It was hoped that the local colonial government authorities would look favourably on its work, and it was vital that everything was done well. While Caroline laboured in Britain, Archibald was working long hours each day in Australia, setting up the system through which people would pay back the money they had been lent by the Society, establishing centres for this in various places.

Emigrant ships were now departing from Britain in substantial numbers, and emigration was rarely out of the news. Into hard-working and busy days Caroline now had the added intrusion of publicity. Her portrait was painted and articles about her appeared in magazines and newspapers.

The 'Money Market and City Intelligence' section of *The Times* in January 1852 carried some correspondence which speculated as to how the Society was prospering financially. Caroline wrote robustly and with characteristic humour to assure readers that all was well: 'Gratifying as it may be to have my name mentioned with praise in *The Times*, still I cannot, as the society's parent, allow my promising and healthy child, which I have reared in the suburbs with so much maternal suffering and privation, to be introduced to the world as having the rickets, or suffering a sickly constitution'. All was indeed well – the Legislative Council of New South Wales during the year voted £10,000 for the furtherance of the aims of the society. This was a substantial vote of confidence in its work, and was chiefly due to the enthusiasm and commitment of the premier, Sir Stuart Donaldson. Born in London in 1812, he had gone to Mexico as a young man and then to Australia. First elected to the Legislative Council in 1848, he was always a firm supporter of Caroline's work.

A further boost of a most practical nature also came from a rich and successful shipowner, Mr W.S. Lindsay. He had long been a campaigner for the cause of shipping reform, having himself worked as a 'ship's boy' when only a teenager. After meeting Caroline, he was inspired to put his energies and talents fully at the service of her emigrants. The result was a ship which was to prove an inspiration and model for many other emigrant ships – the *Caroline Chisholm*, with internal fittings all based specifically on Mrs Chisholm's own instructions. It offered the chance of a healthy and even enjoyable voyage – plenty of storage space, plenty of air, and with the welfare and comfort of passengers as the top priority. It was due to sail in the early part of 1853, heading for Melbourne. By now, Caroline was firmly established in Australian popular culture as the provider of cheerful, hard-working and virtuous girls who would make good Australian wives for waiting men. So there was much interest when the passenger lists were read. The *Melbourne Morning Herald* had some fun with this, referring to 'damsels' who were 'resolved to emigrate to Australia for the noblest and most humanizing of purposes'. Sometimes there was a suggestion that they only wanted to find men who had got rich on the gold-fields.

Caroline still spent a good deal of her time on the detective-work of tracking down missing members of divided families. More and more people who had emigrated or been sent out to Australia as convicts were now, having done well, anxious to send for relatives with whom they had not been in touch for many years. Caroline faithfully attended to every such enquiry. She visited workhouses – or 'unions' as they were commonly called – and found elderly people who had given up a missing son for dead and were overjoyed to find him still alive and anxious to send for them. She found young people who had been left with relatives as children and who could now go out to join their parents. She was particularly anxious to unite the families of those who had gone out in the first heady months of the 'gold rush' of two years previously. Often they had left in haste and not made adequate plans to send for their relatives – this was where her Society could step in to help.

Paperwork was very time-consuming, and while her mother cared for the smallest children, the older boys helped her to answer letters. She was known for her hard work and for the effort that she took with the humblest enquirer. Many of the letters she received were ill-written and with comical spelling. But they represented whole chapters of family history, and the happiness and peace of mind of many individuals.

Shipboard conditions were now improving swiftly, as ship-owners realised that they not only had to comply with the new Passenger Act but must also compete with one another for a new and better-informed class of emigrant who, armed with Mrs Chisholm's information and ideas, was making specific enquiries about facilities before obtaining a berth on board. The whole public perception of emigration was also subtly changing. It was no longer the last resort of the 'ne'er-do-well'. It was becoming the prudent, courageous and exciting decision of the hard-working man who wanted the best for his family. Stories of the Australian colonies in the press tended to feature the emigrant family as enterprising people who were bringing pride to Britain's name.

A biography of Caroline was published, by Trelawney Saunders, to tell the British public more about the woman who was having such an impact on social policy. It told the story in straightforward but moving language: 'Mrs Chisholm is a lady who is not rich, or related to any great people; but she has been engaged nearly all her life in helping labouring and poor people, by teaching them how to help themselves; and she has succeeded so well, that there are thousands who look upon her with feelings of as much affection as if she were their mother.'

The author had certainly managed to get a flavour of Caroline's domestic life: 'She has a husband, who has gone out to Australia lately to help her good work, and six children; from morning until late at night any man or women, or young girl, no matter how humble, how poorly dressed, is welcome to come and consult her, and tell her their griefs. At breakfast, dinner, tea and supper, she is at the command of the unhappy and distressed; and when she is not talking, she is writing letters. For besides all those in England who consult her, hundreds and hundreds of people in Australia send to her to get their relations out to join them. Mrs Chisholm never asks what country or what religion anyone is who comes to her; but she just sets about to see the way of helping them to get out of their difficulties.'

Caroline had never been remotely interested in the kind of 'charity work' which consisted of sitting on a committee for some fashionable cause, and being comfortably far away from any actual social contact with the poor or deprived. Instead, as Saunders pointed out 'She is a lady who had for a long time chosen to abandon the luxuries, even the comforts to which her station entitled her; to wear stuff instead of silk; to work hard; to live hard; to save, that she may spend on the emigrating poor.'

Caroline was still not receiving any salary, and the Islington home was indeed modest. But the friendliness and conviviality of the Monday evening emigrant meetings had communicated itself to a wider audience. Even at the height of her fame, while Saunders' book was on sale in London bookshops and descriptions of her were appearing in widely-read magazines, she remained immersed in her work and never altered her style of living or her approach to people. Her small groups continued, each Monday, to be welcomed at the door by herself or her mother, and to crowd on to the benches in the small room to hear letters from Australia read aloud or be shown the latest design of ship's bunk.

The time was coming when Caroline could take stock of her efforts, and see the possibility of returning with the children to Australia. But their family life was now bound up with the fortunes of the Society which they had founded, and she could not possibly leave England until its future, and the future of emigration generally, was assured. It all took time. Eventually, in August 1852 she was able to write a detailed letter to *The Times* setting out how things stood with regard to her work:

'Until very recently there has been no channel through which the Australian settler could safely and cheaply remit small sums to England.

'When I was resident in Sydney may emigrants were anxious to send small sums to their friends "at home" and came to me with money for that purpose but I found that the banks charged as much as for £15 as for £50 and that they altogether declined to take the trouble of remitting small amounts. On making a representation of this fact to his Excellency Sir George Gipps, he communicated with the banks through the Colonial Secretary, and they consented to receive small remittances from labouring people if I personally accompanied the depositor; but, with my other engagements, it was impossible for me to spare many hours in the week to introducing shepherds and stockmen with their £5 or £10 to the cashiers of banks. Many a man, within my knowledge, has gone away on finding that he could not remit his intended present to his relations, and spent the amount in a drunken "spree". I therefore determined that on my return to England I would endeavour to organise some plan which should render labourers remitting their little tributes of affection to their friends nearly as easy as posting a letter.

'As soon as the Family Colonisation Loan Society was organised, Messrs Coutts and Co. consented to appoint agents and receive the remittance due to the society. But, in order to teach and encourage the labouring colonists to take advantage of the power of remitting to England, my husband saw that it was necessary that some one devoted to the work should proceed to the colonies. The society was not rich enough to pay an agent, or even to pay the expenses of an agent who would work without salary; therefore we determined to divide our income and separate. My husband proceeded to the colony to collect and remit the loans of the society's emigrants, and the savings of those who wished to be joined by parents, other children, brothers, sisters, or other relatives. I remained here to assist such relations to emigrate in an economical, safe, and decent manner, as well as to carry on the correspondence needful for discovering the relatives of long separated emigrants – often a difficult task. We determined to work thus until the labourers' remittances should swell to such an amount as would render it worth the attention of bankers as a matter of business, if the Society were not inclined to continue the trouble and responsibility.

'I am happy to say my faith in the generous and honest disposition of British emigrants, English, Scottish, and Irish, has not been shaken, and that I may look forward with confidence to a very early date when the remittance-connection of the Australian emigrants will be eagerly competed for by the most respected firms ... It is my intention to return to Australia in the early part of next year, and there endeavour to still further promote the reunion of families. I have addressed this letter to your widely-spread and influential columns in order to call the attention of the commercial world to the profits which may be obtained by ministering to a demand which is arising among a humble class – in order to call the attention of statesmen and philanthropists to a new element of peace, order and civilisation, more powerful than soldiers – to a golden chain of domestic feeling, which is bridging the seas between England and Australia ... I shall be prepared to receive the contributions of any persons who generously will lend the gold-diggers and money-getting labourers of Australia the means of being reunited with their families before winter sets in and dooms many of the aged parents "on the roll' to another Christmas dinner in an union.'

As 1853 opened, and news spread of Caroline's plans to return to Australia, magazines and journals began to analyse her work and achievements. The January edition of *The Rambler* carried a review of the Saunders book. Describing Caroline as 'one of the most remarkable women of modern times' the review said that 'Thousands are indebted to her for all that they possess of health, of hope, and of happiness'. It emphasised the enormity of her achievement: 'To estimate the effect of her exertions, two things, however, are necessary. We must understand the nature and extent of those social evils with which she has contended so bravely, and we must become acquainted with the deplorable effects which have resulted from the neglect, on the part of governments and legislatures, of efforts such as those so successfully made by an unassisted individual, and that individual a woman.' Castigating the system of poor-rates and workhouses, it also had harsh words for the crude and ineffective emigration policies which had led to the disaster in Canada in 1847 when hundreds of Irish emigrants died of cholera in overcrowded ships, lacking any medical attention or basic facilities, while they were within sight of the shore on which they had set all their hopes. Mrs Chisholm had set herself to ensure that such horrors had not been repeated with Australian emigration and had been so successful that 'England may yet have to acknowledge that she owes much of the prosperity and perhaps of the permanence of her colonial empire to Mrs Chisholm.'

But before she finally went back to Australia, Caroline was to embark on another major trip, this time to the mainland of Europe. She had some business for the society there, and also had to visit Rome, from where she had had bad news. Young William, who had been doing well in his studies for the priesthood, had been seriously ill. It seemed likely that he would have to leave, and be nursed back to health at home. Now in his late teens, he still had his life's choices ahead of him. He would, it was hoped, be able to travel back with the rest of the family to Australia and make a fresh start there.

In France, Caroline was invited to meet both French and German would-be emigrants, and found that her fame had gone before her. She spoke good French — she had been well taught as a girl back at home with the governess in Northampton — and was able to answer their questions and talk about land prospects and farming in Australia. In Rome, she was granted the privilege of an audience with the Pope, Pius IX. He too knew of her work, and in a brief conversation praised and congratulated her. He also presented her with a gold medal, and with a marble bust of herself, which had been specially commissioned for the occasion.

On her return, Caroline launched into busy preparations for the long trip back to Australia. A huge public rally was held in her honour, at which a number of people paid generous tribute to her work. There was a leading article in *The Times* praising her, and *Punch* also published a poem in her honour. This struck a down-to-earth and merry note, contrasting Caroline's work with that of people who supported other fashionable causes:

'Come all you British females of wealth and high degree
Bestowing all your charity on lands beyond the sea,
I'll point you to a pattern that a better plan with teach
Than that of sending missioners to Timbuctoo to preach.

Converting of the Heathen's a very proper view
By preaching true religion to Pagan and to Jew,
And bringing over Cannibals to Christian meat and bread,

Unless they catch your Parson first and eat him up instead.

But what's more edifying to see, a pretty deal,
Is hearty British labourers partaking of a meal
With wives, and lots of children, about their knees that climb,
And, having tucked their platefuls in, get helped another time.

Beyond the roaring ocean, beneath the soil we tread,
You've English men and women, well housed and clothed and fed,
Who but for help and guidance to leave our crowded shores,
Would now be stealing, begging, or lie starving at our doors.

Who taught them self-reliance, and stirred them to combine
And club their means together, to get across the brine,
Instead of strikes, and mischief, and breaking of the law,
And wasting time in hearing incendiaries jaw?

Who led their expeditions? And under whose command
Through dangers and through hardships sought they the promised land?
A second Moses, surely, it was who did it all,
It was a second Moses in a bonnet and a shawl.'

The poem went on to point out that a public subscription fund had been opened to honour Mrs Chisholm. It urged its readers to be generous in their donations, and pointed out how much had been achieved through emigration:

'By means of one good lady were all these wonders wrought,
By Caroline Chisholm's energy, benevolence, and thought,
Instead of making here and there a convert of a Turk,
She has made idle multitudes turn fruitfully to work.

The ragged pauper crawling home towards a parish grave
She roused − directed to a home beyond the western wave;
She smoothed his weary passage across the troubled deep,
With food and air, and decencies of ship-room and of sleep.

There's many a wife and mother will bless that lady's name,
Embracing a fat infant – who might else have drowned the
same,
A mother, yet no wife, compelled by poverty to sin,
And die in gaol or hospital of misery and gin.

The Reverend Ebenezer I'll not deny his dues,
For saving Patagonians, and Bosjesmen, and Zooloos,
But Mrs Chisholm's mission is what I far prefer;
For saving British natives I'd give the palm to her.

And now that a subscription is opened and begun,
In order to acknowledge the good that she has done
Among that sort of natives – the most important tribe –
Come down like handsome people, and handsomely sub-
scribe'.

And subscribe they did – from prominent Jewish bankers
such as the Rothschilds to Miss Florence Nightingale, from
Lord Canning to backbench Members of Parliament. Nearly
£1,000 was subscribed in all, which would prove to be of great
help to the Chisholms as they were still living only on an Army
pension and the sea journey would be expensive.

Young Archibald had already set off for Australia, in
advance of the rest of the family, to join his father and
to help establish the new family home in New South Wales.
The aim was to allow Captain Chisholm to retire from
the Family Colonisation Society, handing over the work to
others. Caroline would still, of course, be active in helping
newly-arrived emigrants, but it was hoped that there might
be more time for family activities. The little girls were now
just beginning their education, and needed to be provided
for, and the boys too needed help to make their own way
in the world.

Caroline was now very well known as a public speaker –
there had been a 'numerous audience' at the Mechanics
Institute in Greenwich when she spoke in January and huge
attendances at rallies in Liverpool which she had addressed on
the subject of shipping reform – and the prospect of a major
meeting in London held no terrors for her. Nevertheless, it

must have been a little overwhelming to discover just how far her fame had spread, and just how much attention was being paid to her. Held at the London Tavern, the meeting was given great prominence in the next day's edition of *The Times* (Aug 10th). The meeting was under the chairmanship of Northampton's MP, Mr Vernon Smith, who had proved such a great support to her during all these years in England. He spoke of the pride which Northampton felt in Mrs Chisholm and paid warm tribute not only to her energy and enthusiasm but also to the completely non-sectarian nature of her effort. Mr Sidney Herbert also spoke, as did Mr Robert Lowe from Australia. It was an evening to be remembered, and Caroline must have left with the cheers ringing in her ears and with a sense that old antagonisms concerning her religion, and old prejudices against Australia as a wild and dangerous place fit only for convicts, had truly been put away for ever.

Among other tributes to her at this time, *Chambers Journal* published a long eulogy, ending 'She is about to depart, to renew under strange yet favourable auspices her old labours, in colonizing and cultivating the earth, and in civilizing and humanizing the people ... The work before her is heavy, but she is equal to the work. All who wish well to their country and our triple dependencies at the Antipodes, will in full confidence, wish her God-speed'.

Plans for a grand departure in the *Caroline Chisholm* however, were abandoned when that ship was requisitioned for war service in the Crimea. Other ships that Caroline had so carefully ensured were up to a decent standard of accommodation also went the same way, and it was six months later than she planned when she was finally able to sail herself. It was not on the *Caroline Chisholm* but on the *Ballarat* that she finally embarked, with William, Henry, Sydney and little Carry and Monica. The *Illustrated London News* carried a report, noting that there were 167 passengers in all, including a group of Jewish girls. Their presence, incidentally, was a result of concern felt by the Jewish community about the problems of young Jewish men in Australia who could not find wives. This was a cause very much after Caroline's own heart, and she was most happy to be able to help in bringing out girls who would find good partners in the colony. Some newspapers – not without a hint of anti-semitism − sneered at the arrangement, but it endeared Caroline to the Jewish community, and was completely in tune with her own strong feelings about ensuring that help was given to people of every religion who needed it. Describing Caroline's farewell message on the deck of the ship, it was noted that among other affecting scenes, a young Jewish girl embraced Mrs Chisholm in gratitude, calling her 'dear mother'.

Caroline had the sorrow of parting from her own mother now, after several happy years of domesticity together. It seemed unlikely that they would meet again. Mrs Jones could rely on the comfort and care provided by the rest of Caroline's brothers and sisters, now all with good homes of their own to offer her, but it must have been a wrench to separate from this much-loved youngest daughter. Caroline's voice broke down when, in a final speech on board, she referred to having to say goodbye to her mother.

The scene was one which Caroline had viewed before, but in which she was now playing a dramatic personal part. Every emigrant ship represented so many broken ties with home, as well as so much hope. Its bittersweet tone was to be well captured in a contemporary painting *The Last of England* in which a couple were seen gazing from the deck of a ship at the departing shore. Although the ship's reasonable comforts were due in no small part to her own campaigning efforts, although the emigrants on board were people whom she had brought together and helped by encouragement and enthusiasm, although the whole concept of emigration was one in which she wholeheartedly believed, it must still have been with very turbulent emotions that Caroline herself watched the last of England slip away over the horizon as the ship's great sails filled and she swept steadily over the water on the long journey to the other end of the world.

# Chapter Twelve

# Nunc Dimittis

The *Ballarat* docked at Melbourne in July 1854, and a substantial crowd had gathered to welcome Mrs Chisholm. She was warmly cheered when she appeared on deck. The welcome was one which had been long prepared – the Melbourne newspapers had carried news of the ship's impending arrival and there were plenty of people who were eager to show their thanks and affection to the woman who had made such a difference to many lives. But the best welcome must surely have come from the two Archibalds, father and son, who were waiting for her with a carriage and who escorted her and the children off to the new family home in Flinders Lane.

It was a modest enough home. Following the completion of his work with the Family Colonisation Society, which had now been safely delivered into other hands, Archibald had started a small business, specialising in selling provisions to people who were going to the goldfields. Chisholm and Son was not a very large enterprise, but it had a warehouse and a base from which to operate, and Archibald was already looking ahead to investment in some of the other projects that were to be started in the colony – including even a railway.

There was a more formal welcome home a few weeks later, with a public meeting at Melbourne's Mechanics Institute. Just as Caroline had been sent off from London with good wishes, speeches, and kindly messages of thanks and goodwill, now she was being welcomed back to Australia in the same spirit. It all helped to open the next chapter of her life happily.

The next few years were to prove a mixture of domestic responsibilities and of continuing labour on behalf of other families. Australia had changed dramatically in the years that Caroline had been away. It now had not only a substantially enlarged population, but more roads, larger townships, and whole new forms of industry and commerce that had grown up as a result of the gold rush. The Chisholms remained in Melbourne for some time, and later moved to Kyneton. Caroline visited the goldfields, and started to become involved with some of the issues facing the country. She launched the idea of 'shelter sheds' along the main highways – substantial but simple buildings; with wood and water provided, in which people on long journeys could spend the night. These were to prove a great boon to many travellers. Sometimes they were known as 'Chisholm's Shakedowns'. Later, she opened a small school, in which her own Carry and Monica were among the pupils. Her advice and opinions were sought on many issues, and she spoke up for the small farmers and for those who wanted to buy small plots of land and start for themselves.

There were sorrows to come. William, having had to abandon the ideas of the priesthood, settled in Melbourne and eventually went into business. Later, when the rest of the family moved to Kyneton he sent the happy news that he was engaged to be married. The wedding took place at St Francis church in 1855 and the ceremony was performed by the local bishop. But, sadly, William's health had continued to be very poor. He died only three years later, leaving his young widow with a small baby. To complete the tragedy, the child died only a few months later. Young Mrs Chisholm later entered a convent.

William's death came at a time when the family was also undergoing severe financial difficulties. Archibald's various business enterprises were never very successful, and Caroline contracted a kidney disease. Later, when she had recovered – though she was never from then on to enjoy really good health – she emerged into public life again, giving occasional lectures. By this time the family had moved to Sydney – where the whole adventure of her work with settlers had begun. Sydney was now a completely different city, with gold having brought enormous prosperity resulting in the erection of many fine buildings. It was here that she re-opened her school, which had been closed for a time because of her illness.

Eventually, young Henry Chisholm also married, and settled into a home of his own. The girls were now in their late teens.

Major Chisholm – he had been given this rank on official retirement from the Indian Army and had generally used it in Australia – was now growing old. A decision was taken to go home to England and finish the girls' education there.

The years of public welcomes, rallies, and meetings were now over. The family settled quietly at Liverpool. But Caroline had not been quite forgotten, and was in due course granted a Civil List pension of £100 a year. This, and the Army pension, was enough on which to live in modest circumstances. Later, both young Archibald and Sydney returned to Australia, and married there. The two Chisholm girls, after attending convent schools in England and in Belgium, also made their own lives. Carry married Edmund Gray, who later became Mayor of Dublin, and Monica was later to go to Canada and marry there.

The last years of Caroline's life were spent in London – first at Highgate Hill and then later at Fulham, where the Chisholms made a home at 43a Barclay Road. Both Carry and Monica were dedicated to their mother, and looked after her during what proved to be long years of illness. She had never really recovered from the kidney disease contracted in Australia, and was confined to bed for most of the late 1860s and the 1870s. The end came on March 25th 1877, after Caroline had been suffering from severe bronchitis for about a forthnight. She died at home, with a Dr Veriton in attendance. It was the Feast of the Annunciation – an appropriate day for one who had been so devoted both to her religion and to the cause of family life.

The family – Carry by this time was married and Monica had been living at home and nursing her mother – arranged for the funeral to take place in Northampton. Major Chisholm was himself too ill to attend. There was considerable publicity both in Northampton papers and in the national press. The Northampton papers noted the details of the ceremony, which took place in the town's imposing new pro-cathedral, some distance away from Holy Sepulchre church where Caroline had been baptised and married. The funeral was conducted by the Revd Bernard Murray. *The Tablet* of April 7th also carried a report: 'FUNERAL OF MRS CAROLINE CHISHOLM – The remains of this philanthrophic lady, wife of Major Chisholm, of Fulham, and well know as "The Emigrant's Friend" were interred in the Cemetery, Northampton, on Saturday last. In accordance with her wish, she was buried in the cemetery just outside Northampton. The remains were removed from town on Friday, and were on their arrival at Northampton received in the Catholic Cathedral there by the Bishop of Northampton. The funeral took place shortly after noon, the chief mourners being Miss Chisholm and Mr Gray. Major Chisholm, the husband of the deceased, lies prostrate with serious illness at Fulham. Many of the townsfolk showed their respect for the memory of the deceased lady by assembling round the grave, into which were thrown numerous bouquets.'

Another Catholic newspaper, *The Universe*, had been founded not long before and also reported the news of Caroline's death. The paper was evidently anxious that the fact of her Catholic faith should be better known. It quoted a letter sent in by a correspondent whose names were given only as 'B': 'Let us hope that the life of so truly good a lady as Mrs Chisholm will be given to the public in a volume. Is it not true that Mrs Chisholm was a Catholic? Protestantism boasts of its John Howard and the Society of Friends of its Mrs Fry; it is only fair that Catholics should speak of one to was the equal to either.'

Over the years Caroline Chisholm's remarkable life has indeed been recorded in various forms − Australia has seen a number of books and even a play about her, and in the 1960s it was decided to depict her on a banknote, the 5-dollar note, as a testimony to the role she occupied in Australian history. Alas, she does not appear on the new (1992) version. In Britain, although her fame lingered in the 19th century, especially in Northampton, she gradually faded from the public memory. In 1917 there was a brief revival of interest when a little pamphlet about her was published by the Catholic Truth Society − perhaps fulfilling that plea made in *The Universe* at the time of her death.

In recent years the fame of Mrs Chisholm has revived to some extent. In the 1970s a new Catholic girls school in Australia was named after her. The school, in Regentville, has the motto 'Faith, Courage and Tolerance' and is run by the Schoenstatt sisters. Its prospectus issued to parents says 'Caroline Chisholm High School, established in 1974, is a Regional Catholic Girls High School serving the parishes of Emu Plains, Kingswood, Penrith, and Warragamba.' After a brief resume of the life of Caroline Chisholm, it goes on 'You will all agree that the qualities shown by Caroline Chisholm make her a worthy model for your daughter to emulate and it has been decided that the school motto should commemorate these qualities.' The school even has a song:

> 'Caroline Chisholm, great woman of faith!
> You promised to know neither country nor creed
> But only to serve God's people in need
> For this you sacrificed wishes and feelings
> Surrendered all comfort, for your work and mission.'

In 1976 the Catholic Bishops of Australia issued this prayer, to be used by people who had been particularly inspired by Caroline Chisholm:

> 'Heavenly Father, in your boundless love you provide for your people. In the person of Caroline Chishom you cared for the women of this growing nation and implanted here a concern for the dignity of womanhood. Let her life of selfless concern be a model and an inspiration for Christian people today. We ask this through Christ Our Lord . . .'

There have even been some suggestions that Caroline Chisholm might one day be formally canonised by the Catholic Church as a saint. For this, a lengthy procedure is necessary, entailing a careful checking of everything she ever wrote and did.

History has rolled on and seems to have swept Australia's colonial past into the far distance. If you stand in modern Sydney today among the office blocks shimmering in the sun, watching people rush to work or the traffic streaming out towards the suburbs or the beach, it is very hard to imagine the tents and wooden shacks of one and a half centuries ago. Similarly, the London that Caroline Chisholm knew has changed beyond recognition. But the church where she worshipped − St John's in Islington − still stands and is the heart of a busy parish, and in Northampton her grave is kept clean and tidy in the Billings Road cemetery. In 1990 the *Northants Herald and Post* ran a feature on Caroline under the heading 'Emigrants' Saviour'. On the centenary of her death (1977) questions were asked in the Victoria State Parliament in Melbourne about the condition of her grave, and when this was reported back in England the parish priest of St Gregory's church in Northampton himself went to the cemetery to give it a good scrub. Since then it has regularly been cleaned and kept in good order — most recently a group of children from St David's school were photographed cleaning it up following a geography lesson in which they had learned about Australia and Mrs Chisholm.

The values for which Caroline stood — family unity, patriotism, a sense of God's providence and a willingness to make His blessings available to everyone — are still essential today. Her conviction that people should be encouraged to work hard to provide for their relatives makes the same sense today as it did when she expounded it in the last century. Her deep Catholic faith, upheld in the face of considerable pressure, was a source of strength and joy to her all her life and it was this faith, and not a political or philosophical conviction, which inspired her tremendous work. These are all points to ponder in considering her life. We also owe to her the great historical achievement of the links between Britain and Australia — links which to this day bring hundreds of families together as grandparents make the long journey to be reunited with their families on the other side of the world.

Today's Australians are profoundly conscious of the fact that their country welcomes immigrants from all over the world. After the Second World War the country opened itself to refugees from every corner of Europe. After the Vietnam War thousands of 'boat people' found a home there. A favourite Australian boast is that Melbourne is the largest Greek city in the world after Athens. Another boast is of the variety and quality of restaurants to be found in all the country's major cities. All of this has helped to dilute the sense of a particular link with Britain and to make the folk-memory of a ship seeing the 'last of England' very distant. But a country's history has deeper riches than may at first appear. Caroline Chisholm's emigrants brought with them an understanding of the need for helping one another, a love of family, and a sense of self-worth which all became embedded in the country's very fabric. These are messages worth passing on to every new generation.

Finally, in an age when women's roles have been much discussed, and the place of women in history has been the subject of considerable study, the life of Caroline Chisholm gives us a different perspective. It challenges us by reminding us that a woman was able to achieve much even in the days when women did not vote in elections and when their family duties were seen as paramount. This achievement was possible for a woman prepared to dedicate herself wholeheartedly to a worthwhile cause with a strong sense of being answerable before God. In such a case, a family can be an inspiration and support, and in no way a hindrance to other work. Today, both in Britain and Australia, Caroline Chisholm's words on subjects such as God, marriage, women, crime, work, family ties and everyday duties strike a challenging note. Her views may irritate people who prefer a less robustly Christian approach. Perhaps we should ask ourselves whether our own achievements will stand the test of time as hers have done, and whether our motivation is as generous and open-hearted as hers so evidently was.

Today we do not need to battle against filthy emigrant ships, rats, or bullying sea-captains. But we face problems of family break-up, a rising tide of crime, and a concern that modern consumerism is creating ecological problems that may prove very hard to conquer. Perhaps a share in Caroline Chisholm's robust optimism, based on a real sense of God's providence, and a conviction that with common sense and goodwill all sorts of difficulties can be overcome, would be good for us all.

# Conclusion

Why should people today be interested in a woman who lived over a hundred years ago, in the wholly different world of Queen Victoria's reign and the emerging British Empire?

Australia has changed beyond all recognition from the collection of colonies that Caroline Chisholm knew. Most of its citizens — who come from every continent and among whom those of British origin are by no means any longer the most dominant in many groups and organisations — live in big modern cities. Their lifestyles are far removed from those of the rural settlers whose cause Caroline championed so staunchly.

To Caroline Chisholm, a nation's chief resource was not its gold or the richness of its soil, its harbours or its sea-lanes, but its people. She sought to encourage people to have faith in their own courage, resilience, independence of spirit, and desire to succeed. This sort of far-sighted acceptance of the potential of the human spirit is still very much needed today.

Today, in both Australia and Britain, our communal life is more fragmented than it was in the nineteenth century. We have come to believe that we ought to be able to live as private units, sharing no common sense of purpose and requiring little mutual support or encouragement at the practical level most of the time. A good look at the way the Australian nation came into being reveals an exhilarating mixture of both gritty independence and strong mutual support. It is this mixture which can produce long-lasting and important results.

Caroline Chisholm championed not the great nationalised enterprise but the little, independent emigrant and his family. This approach achieved far more than the grandiose concepts of other planners, many of whom thought in terms of exploiting resources such as gold or wool rather than populating a countryside and building up a nation.

Family life is not as optional as many in this generation would have us believe. It is a source of strength, a safeguard for the vulnerable, a rich resource of affection and enthusiasm and encouragement. Yet today many families fragment, and many children grow up not knowing the stability of a home where two parents, married for life, raise a family as a common unit.

Caroline was able to take the idea of the family for granted, but had to struggle against those who refused families the help and support necessary to thrive during a harsh sea journey or on arrival in a raw new land. Today, we perhaps need to defend the family's very essence − but in doing so we can use much of her common sense, her practicality, her belief in the human capacity to overcome problems and to achieve. We can also usefully learn from her sincere but never dogmatic religious beliefs: her mixture of tolerance with deeply held convictions which were unfashionable at the time but which she did not change. She was clearly a woman of great spiritual resources, and she succeeded in passing on her Catholic faith to her children in such a way that their subsequent lives were similarly moulded and formed by it. She had to face taunts because of her adherence to a Church which was often misrepresented to her fellow countrymen, but she did not waver. Today, believers face different but equally ugly taunts, and could usefully follow her example, which was one of such courteous generosity of spirit that insults withered and were replaced by genuine respect.

Through Caroline's efforts, many Australian settlers achieved a home and some land of their own at a time when many back in Britain and Ireland could never hope to own property. She established Australian life on a basis of homes and families, a heritage which was perhaps taken for granted by several following generations but which today needs to be appreciated anew.

We often sneer at our Victorian ancestors, whose language and code of living seems so at variance with what fashion now dictates as right. This can become a smug and narrow-minded way of looking at our heritage. Perhaps it is now time to face history with honesty and pay tribute where it is due. Mrs Chisholm's achievement has stood the test of time better than that of many whose efforts have been hailed with greater honour and fame.

# Bibliography

*Fifty One Pieces of Wedding Cake* – Mary Hoban, Lowden Publishing Co, Australia, 1973.
*Caroline Chisholm* – Margaret Kiddle, Melbourne University Press, 1957.